"Joan is always a bright spot in your day. She touches your heart AND your funny bone, and makes you remember to not sweat the small stuff. Great writer, great speaker, great inspiration, and great friend."

Mark Mayfield, National Speakers Association Hall of Fame

"Some people are simply nutritious in that they are good for your very being. Joan is such a person as she continues to share life's lessons with grace and unique perspectives."

Lawrence L. Grypp, President, Goering Center for Family and Private Business at the University of Cincinnati

"Joan inspires all that are touched by her. Through Joan's insights we are given a crystal clear view of the beauty and the blessings in the world around us."

Ronald Price, Senior Vice President, Chief Marketing Officer CLA, American National Insurance Company

"Joan's words are as inspiring as her life. You'll love this book!"

Dewitt Jones Keynote speaker/National Geographic Photographer

"The depth of emotion Joan exposes in her writing gives the reader combined humor and tears. If you thought you are limited to the five senses—you have not read what Joan Brock has to offer."

Chuck Wall, Ph.D., Founder KindnessUSA.Org

"I have known, admired, and loved Joan for two decades. I have seen her move audiences of thousands from laughter to tears and then, back to laughter. Her enormous wit, humor, and reverence for life shines through in all she does. I will be passing her new book on to everyone I know."

Mimi Donaldson, speaker/author

"Joan Brock is the most inspirational person I have ever met. Do yourself a favor and read this wise and wonderful book."

Mary LoVerde, Author, The Invitation

"Joan's life was literally, physically, and emotionally in darkness. But through her great faith she gathered a renewed sight from her soul, shining her love onto everyone she encounters. There is no greater grace than the courage, strength, and wisdom that she shares with us.

Deacon Jim Knipper, St. Paul Catholic Church, Princeton, New Jersey (James J. Knipper, President/CEO, J. Knipper and Company, Inc, Lakewood, New Jersey)

"This book is inspiring because Joan herself is so inspiring. Wisdom about using YOUR senses leaps off the page, because of her own experience. She applies what she has learned so powerfully; you won't be able to put this book down."

Bert Decker, Founder and CEO, Decker Communications, Inc., Author of You've Got To Be Believed To Be Heard

TO YOUR COME SENSES

AN INSPIRATIONAL GUIDE FOR USING ALL OF YOUR SENSES

JOAN BROCK

Come to Your Senses:
An Inspirational Guide for Using All of Your Senses

Published by Wheatmark®
1760 East River Road, Suite 145, Tucson, Arizona 85718 U.S.A.
www.wheatmark.com

ISBN: 978-1-60494-884-4 (paperback)
ISBN: 978-1-60494-885-1 (ebook)
LCCN: 2012947719

All Scripture quotations unless indicated otherwise have been taken from the King James Version of the Holy Bible.

DEDICATION

For my All-American Butterfly Man
Always for my Joy and her Brian
And now for my new grandson Skyler!

IN MEMORY OF

My beloved mother, Vivian Stuebbe

May 5, 1926 – June 23, 2011
Mom, we will always miss you.

CONTENTS

FOREWORD

It's been said that when someone loses his or her vision, the other senses compensate by becoming more acute. In the case of Joan Brock, who lost her vision over the course of just three short weeks, it wasn't just her other four physical senses that stepped up to meet her new challenges, but rather a cornucopia of other senses as well.

I first met Joan ten years ago, after reading her compelling memoir, *More Than Meets The Eye*, and contacted her to see if she'd be interested in letting me tell her story as a television movie. I was immediately struck by how this woman, whose world had become a monochromatic blur of gray shadows, was able to "see" so much color in the world, and share so much of her own inner light. As an inspirational speaker, Joan delights in the fact that "It took me going blind to see the world!" Indeed, her talks have taken her around the world, speaking alongside such notable personalities as Henry Kissinger and Benazir Bhutto.

After making *More Than Meets The Eye: The Joan Brock Story* for Lifetime Television, I worked with Joan on her early ideas for this book. Just as she had shown me so much with her first book about honor, grace, and humor, with *Come To Your Senses* Joan showed me how limited a quintessential life really was: So many other "senses," I quickly learned, were not only quietly woven into each of our own personalities, but were ripe for developing, enhancing, and sharing, in order to more fully engage with our fellow man.

I am thrilled to see this inspiring book come to fruition. Each chapter continues to surprise me with simple insights about life, as observed through senses beyond the five physical ones, reminding me how enriched my own journey has been since the day this remarkable woman came into my life. It is with a profound sense of gratitude and sense of honor that I invite you to sit back, open your mind and your heart, and... *Come to Your Senses.*

Michael Bremer, Executive Producer, *More Than Meets The Eye: The Joan Brock Story*

INTRODUCTION

And So It Began . . .

Going blind was nothing . . . compared to experiencing my young husband dying of cancer. During the many long, difficult nights of struggling through these extraordinary events, I was never alone. Even in the darkest of hours, I somehow crawled out of that valley and found the light of day because God was by my side.

I'm an ordinary person to whom extraordinary things have happened. Growing up as a minister's daughter, I learned many life lessons, not only in Sunday school but while sitting at the family dinner table. My childhood proved to be instrumental in helping me pull through the tough times.

I also believe I received a version of therapy before my traumatic events. During the different stages of my life, I have been able to retrieve my memories and use them to bring me through it all. It's important to note, however, that

1

I'm not special. Only through my family, my friends, my experiences, and my faith did I begin to realize that my blindness gave me unfathomable knowledge. Through a myriad of life lessons, I became more aware of the multitude of senses anyone can tap into, thus completing the whole picture of life.

I have often been asked how I got through the loss of my sight at age thirty-two and then the loss of my husband only five years later. To answer that, I've had to closely evaluate things. Where *did* the strength come from to survive and eventually thrive? I can say that none of it came without hard work, immense sadness, and buckets full of laughter . . . and all of it came with help from my rock-solid friends, family, and faith.

So often, swirling thoughts going through my head have me reliving what happened. The first time I kept going back to was one wintry Iowa day when I was peering in my daughter Joy's dresser drawer, looking for her small pink socks. I could see the variety of colors, but where were the ones I needed?

"Joy? Where are your pink socks?" I asked as my beautiful three-year-old bounced into the room. Joy walked over, reached in, and quickly handed them to me.

"Here, Mommy, these are pink," Joy said matter of factly. She walked back to her bed, leaned back, and held up her wiggling feet for me to put on the socks.

As I looked at them, they were white, not pink.

Puzzled, I cautiously continued gathering the socks in my hands and proceeded dressing my daughter. Yet, a second clue happened that very afternoon. The fluorescent lighting in my office at the school for blind children made me squint. I had to put on sunglasses.

Yes, while working at a school for blind children, I lost my sight. How could this be? Having been on staff at the school for the previous five years, I had become a certified brailist and filled a variety of positions. What better preparation could I have had?

I lost my sight within the next three weeks—no warning given! What had happened? I had contracted a rare autoimmune condition that entered my system, attacked my eyes, and rapidly turned my life inside out.

During the subsequent hospitalization, the seemingly hundreds of tests explained the autoimmune disease that attacked my veins and cells going to the retina. The disease stealthily destroyed my cones and rods, creating a condition similar to macular degeneration.

"Joan, we have finally discovered a few things from the test results," said Dr. Corbett, the lead doctor for my case. Having just had the first of several spinal taps, I lay flat and motionless. He again began to talk, frequently using terminology that meant nothing to me. Then came a moment when his words rang loud and clear . . .

"Joan, the damage we see to your retina is rare. We actually have never seen it before, particularly in such a short period of time and for such a young person. In fact, you're the only one in the country we can find who has ever had this kind of deterioration."

My senses went numb. A slow, sick feeling filled my body. I had to clear my mind to absorb the news. What could be worse? I felt a need to pray. "God, oh God, help me!" I didn't want to hear any more words.

Then he spoke again, very slowly. "We also believe the damage we're seeing is irreversible."

My mind whirled. Not only could I not move, I couldn't think. My first clear thoughts centered on the word *irreversible. That means I will never see my daughter's face again?*

How does one process the finality of the words *never — irreversible — forever?*

I felt confused, my hands trembling and my fingers fidgeting with the sheets. I didn't want anyone to see how scared I was. I wanted to be strong, but I wasn't. With open eyes, I lay looking at the ceiling, but I couldn't see it. Would I *ever* see it? Am I staring at a future of visual silence?

During those most difficult moments, though, the foundation of my youth came into my mind, front and center. In my deepest despair, a verse memorized from the Heidelberg Catechism comforted me, that "without the will of my Father in heaven, not a hair can fall from my head."

❦

After my vision loss, I continued to work with the blind children for almost five more years. In retrospect, those students proved to be an encouraging force. And at my fingertips were immediate training, support, and guidance from those fore mentioned friends, staff, and family.

My sense of peace, I realized, would ultimately come through my own acceptance and through integrating into my own life the techniques I'd been teaching. My husband Joe was the recreation director and assistant administrator at the school, and he was instrumental in assisting me in our personal world. Young Joy quickly developed insights we could never have imagined. As a family, we went forward in a positive direction as seamlessly as possible, experiencing this new reality task by task, day by day. We were coping well . . . until the other shoe dropped.

It was a hot and sticky July day in Iowa. Joy, age seven, was playing in the schoolyard across the street. I was home. Joe was at a doctor's office having tests run on his ever-troubling sinuses. The phone rang.

"Joan?"

"Hi, Honey, where are you? I thought you'd be home by now."

"I am calling from a pay phone at a truck stop."

"What? Where? Why?"

"I'm on my way to the University of Iowa hospital. I have cancer."

A horrific, heavy silence hung at both ends of the line. I finally spoke.

"Joe, are they sure?"

"I have a vial with a sample of the tissue from the biopsy of my sinuses that they want me to take to the university immediately." The sound of silence again permeated our world. "I'll be home after a while."

"Joe, we'll beat this, too."

"I've got to get going. I have cancer, Joan." His voice seemed calm, resolved, but strangely distant.

"I love you, Joe."

"I know. Call my folks."

Tears dampened my cheeks as I heard the phone line humming at my shoulder. Through my pounding heart, I could only pray for God to help us.

At that moment, Joy ran into the house with her boundless energy.

"Mommy? Are you okay?"

"Yes." I lied as I wiped my face.

"Can I go over to Hillary's house and play?"

"Sure. Just stay out in the yard where I can hear you."

"Okay," she said, and with childlike innocence, skipped out the door.

After making the distressing calls to family, I put down the phone, walked over to the couch, and sat down. Again, I felt numb, sick, confused, and worried—and that helpless feeling, the fear of the unknown. I couldn't think clearly except to wonder what might be going on in Joe's mind. The indescribable tension paralyzed me. I wanted to be with him, hug him, *and fix this*!

This struggle with cancer truly put life in the proper perspective.

Joe received a diagnosis of a rare and aggressive cancer of the sinuses. A week later, he endured a radical procedure—a sixteen-and-a-half-hour surgery—to remove a tumor. He bravely went through radiation and chemo, but tragically, seven months after his surgery, my husband Joe died. He was only thirty-six.

Now I had to face the realization that going blind was nothing compared with fighting this devastating disease and its aftermath. Strangely, it was during Joe's terrible cancer and death that I finally faced the brutal truth. I really *was* blind. My husband really *did* die.

How could I step up and lead my life without the right-hand assistance of my husband? The insightful eyes I'd relied on were gone. I had thought I had *it* all figured out, that my blindness would be the "big deal" in our lives, and that's it. Not so. This new reality shocked and alarmed me.

૪

As the days slowly advanced into months, I had hundreds of decisions to make. I knew I had to open my world to fulfill my role as mother and be a whole person. Many long nights in meditation led me to decisions that changed our lives in ways we could never have foreseen.

After Joy finished second grade, she and I packed our belongings and moved back to the town of my childhood, Bakersfield, California. I knew family and friends from my youth would supply the physical source of comfort and cushion the emotional healing for both of us. During what I call the "rebuilding years," I journaled everything that had happened, beginning with the moment of the pink socks. And of course, I focused on being Joy's mom, taking each moment step by step.

During this time, I took talking computer classes for the blind, and I kept journaling. I rekindled friendships with people from my youth and sat in the pews of the church I'd grown up in. The familiarity of that building, the smell of the sanctuary, even the special feeling of the four walls enveloped me like a warm blanket and calmed my soul—all instrumental in my healing. So was reliving those moments of pain and tragedy. It was not only cleansing but it allowed me to place the realities of what had happened into the proper files in my head.

🜚

A few years after we moved to California, a birthday party set the scene for an important moment in my life. There, I re-met someone very special. Jim Brock was a former high school classmate who'd become an entomologist specializing in butterflies. As we began dating and eventually married, he brought laughter, color, light, and a sense of peace back into my life—and Joy's life, too. I'd been filled with doubt that a happy future with someone other than Joe could ever happen. But I took a chance and allowed my heart to reopen. What an unexpected gift!

🜚

At the time of this writing, I've been blind for more than twenty-eight years and have happily led a positive and productive life. During my rebuilding years, journaling became a cathartic and therapeutic friend. Reliving and studying these life experiences assisted me in going forward and creating this life I'm enjoying today.

In 1994, my life's journal was published as my autobiography, *More Than Meets the Eye,* with coauthor Derek L. Gill. In 2003, a made-for-television film starring Carey Lowell based on that book premiered on Lifetime TV. Since then, I've shared my story hundreds of times as an inspirational speaker, a career that has literally and miraculously taken me around the world. While I wouldn't wish my losses on anyone, my journey through a sightless world and the evolution of living as a blind woman has blessed me with extraordinary insights. I believe they can only have come from feeling fully accepted through the HELP of that all important support system.

Constantly re-evaluating the vast array of senses has become increasingly important to me over the years. Now when I meet people, because I can't judge them visually, I'm blessed to meet them from the inside out. My first impression comes through their energy, their voices, their handshakes, and other signals received through multiple senses. It's a facet of my life that I cherish!

Yes, as humans, we're *more* than our sense of sight. But how do all of our senses make us who we are? That question became the catalyst for *Come to Your Senses.*

This book entertains you with stories from my life that have made twenty-one senses come alive. It also encourages you to examine how each of *your* senses relates to a bigger world—"Our World"—through a special segment in each chapter. And it challenges you to relate to your own experiences through the "Insights to Your Senses" segment.

Tapping into *all* of your senses and examining them closely is your task at hand. From your sense of sight to a sense of peace and from your sense of humor to a sense of loss, know that the wealth you possess within is enormous. When you use your full range of senses, you are completing the whole picture, reaching your full potential, and experiencing your true happiness.

Through laughter, tears, insights, realizations, and thought-provoking lessons, *Come to Your Senses* helps you stop and listen to what your vast number of senses offer. Begin *your* journey of listening, choosing wisely, and re-evaluating how to come to your own senses so you can get through the toughest stuff you'll ever face.

PART I

The Senses We Know

A. The Physical Senses

Sense of Sight

"Keep your face to the sunshine and you cannot see the shadow.
It's what sunflowers do."
— Helen Keller

I have a childhood memory of crawling onto the back
window shelf of our Ford during a late night thirty-min-
ute drive home from my uncle's home. Feeling tired, I'd
wanted space away from my long-legged older brothers,
Bob and Jon. As I snuggled up on that shelf, I could stare
at the billions of sparkling stars in the midnight sky.
Lulled by the relaxing motion of the car, I pondered this
sky peppered with lights. Thoughts and questions swirled
in my mind. *What are these twinkling lights doing? Where will
I be some day and what will I be doing? Is a special person I'd
someday love looking at these stars, too?* This safe, sentimen-
tal moment branded itself into my soul.

Many years later, I moved to South Dakota to attend
college, then remained to start my first recreational therapist job at a state mental hospital and correctional facility.
One night, in the company of a friend who was an amateur

astronomer and several others on staff, we went stargazing on the rolling plains. The only glow in the beautifully clear night came from the radiant stars that reached all the way to the horizon. Our exuberant astrologer pointed out the different constellations hanging in the heavens. He told stories as he pointed out the Big Dipper, the Milky Way, and many others. I got lost in this beautiful sight. Suddenly, I flashed back to snuggling in the back window of the family Ford and those same questions surfaced all over again. *What are these twinkling lights doing up there? Where will I be some day and what will I be doing?* Feelings of wonder, safety, and comfort filled my heart.

During my hospitalization ten years later, the procedures, medications, and overriding confusion caused many sleepless nights. To get through the long hours, I allowed myself to relive my memories. These two starlit nights provided a special place to go to in my mind. Curled up in this comfort, I could let go of my fear and confusion. I feel blessed to have seen the stars and much, much more.

How I treasure the sights I've been given through these memories.

❧

A heightened awareness of this precious jewel's importance—my sense of sight—began in the late '70s. That's when, five years before my own vision loss, I started working at the residential school for blind children in Iowa. My college degree allowed me to have a position supervising employees who'd been working there for years. *They* knew what to do with the ten blind boys under my wing; *I* had no clue. So both the students and the well-trained staff began teaching *me* how to teach *them*. I had no technical skills on getting a blind child to put toothpaste on the tooth-brush or showing a young boy how to walk up and down stairs safely or instructing him on how to make his bed. But I found these learning experiences refreshing, fulfilling, and even exciting. Little did I know how important they'd be for my own future.

In some respects, our blind students were like average children who simply needed to learn skills for becoming accepted socially. As an example, one day, I approached three of the students in my charge as they were talking, laughing, and just being boys in the hallway. One boy faced inward; one stood with his shoulder pointed to the middle of the trio; the third had his back to the other two. They'd taken the attitude that because they could hear one another, why bother facing each other? To me, they resem-bled three bowling pins knocked askew.

In our society, people communicate most effectively when they can look into another person's eyes as they speak. Eye contact often gauges how genuine, confident, and trustworthy someone might be. To become produc-tive citizens in the sighted world, our students needed to practice appropriate eye contact. Often, they had to be told to direct themselves physically to the voice of the person speaking. So on this occasion, I calmly reminded the boys to face one another and quietly moved on.

Don't ever forget that vision is an amazing gift of information that relays the smallest details. A myriad of tidbits fill your senses to create a complete picture. Even a simple facial expression can communicate a lot. For example, while sitting in a meeting, you may look across a large conference table into the eyes of a colleague and, with a slight movement or a roll of the eyes, convey a great idea or express boredom.

It's been said that your sense of sight gives you 80 percent of your information every waking minute, and that your vision supplies a huge portion of your daily needs for functioning and communicating. As you walk into a room, your sight immediately tells you where the furniture stands and how each piece is arranged. Without consciously thinking about it, in a split second, this information feeds into your brain. As you sit down near a window, your peripheral vision catches a bird flying by. You may not actually turn to look, but your side vision has given you feedback with no thought on your part. These kinds of movements stimulate your entire system.

The lyrics of the famous song "The Look of Love" (Burt Bacharach and Hal David, 1967) is filled with connections to one another that "looking" creates. I propose that most of the world has experienced the precious feeling and joy of the look of love in someone's eyes.

For human beings, the eyes take in valuable information from day one. When newborn babies look into the smiling eyes of their mothers, they see candles of learning filled with wishes for joy, understanding, and happiness. Babies mirror their mothers' eyes; that's how they learn to smile. Thus begins "the look of love."

꒷

Yes, the eyes are the windows to your soul. But more than that, the eyes give you the window of what the world has to offer. In my early years of vision loss, I couldn't help but ask, "How could I ever compensate for that immense loss?"

Today, do I miss seeing the stars? Do I wish I could see my daughter's face? Would I enjoy knowing what my new friends look like? Would I like to be able to give my husband "the look of love"? Of course. I have difficult days as you do. Tears fill my eyes thinking of what I miss and the losses I've endured. I am only human.

However, during these moments, I again find myself falling into the memories that have blessed me and helped me heal. They've been my "weapons of choice" in battling the sadness I feel.

I also know that, because of losing my eyesight, I have gained the ability to tap deeply into my other senses, which are described throughout this book. I've realized how all of this has helped me broaden my perspective of life—an extraordinary benefit.

I now live in Tucson, Arizona, where the early morning hours provide a precious time in nature for me. Stepping outside with my morning coffee, I know I'm looking north toward the Santa Catalina Mountains. As the rising sun brings the day's first light, the silhouette of the rustic mountains comes into my extremely limited view. In this quiet, reflective time, I "see" God on His throne and He helps me start my day. As George Washington Carver, American scientist, botanist, educator, and inventor, said, "I love to think of nature as an unlimited broadcasting station, through which God speaks to us every hour, if only we will tune in."

Sense of Sight in Our World

Our world is filled with millions of people who have no physical sight, yet have immense *in*sight into leading a full life. They are skilled lawyers and entertainers, top professors and teachers, wonderful mothers and fathers, fabulous cooks and incredible scholars, who happen to be blind. And they inspire and teach us so much. Their strength, tenacity, and drive influence the world in a positive way and show us what we might strive to achieve.

Words used in conversation often relate to the sense of sight. For example, whether sighted or blind, people talk about *seeing* what someone means; they have *insights* of certain facets of their life; they create *visions of* their future. Indeed, I often say "let's watch television" or "see you later!" Although some people feel uncomfortable using these phrases around me, I'm not offended (nor do I believe are most blind people). Opening our eyes to the knowledge of what works and what's truly offensive (and what's not) moves us toward being a full society of *abilities,* not disabilities. The goal is to become more in tune with the strengths and capabilities of the visually impaired. When that happens, misconceptions will fade away and we'll all feel more comfortable interacting with each other.

Insights into Your Sense of Sight

Your childhood visual memories have been instrumental in creating who you are, as they have been for me. Without totally comprehending what each event puts into your psyche, sight plays an enormous part in feeding information into your being.

What memories have blessed your earliest thoughts? How did your sight play a role in creating a vision you treasure? I recently asked my good friend Connie these questions. "Hmm," she replied, then paused for a long moment. "I would have to think about that, Joan. *You've* been forced into thinking about stuff like this while the rest of us just take our sight for granted."

From this moment on, I charge you with truly appreciating and celebrating your sight, thus honoring this precious gift. Take a moment to concentrate on the most beautiful sight you have ever seen; paint that picture in your mind's eye.

Just as I looked at the stars as a little girl, think of a memory that your sight gave to you when you were young. Ask people around you the same question, allowing the memory of that moment—how it was seen and felt—

to float to the surface. Then share these moments with friends and loved ones. You'll find the experience both thought-provoking and wonderful. And clinging to these memories will help you get through the darkest of days you may ever face. No one can take them from you.

When you closely examine your sight and all of the information it gives, you'll no longer take this sense for granted. Indeed, you'll want to share these experiences with those around you. Whether you're studying the movement of the tiniest insects or standing at the ocean viewing the endless horizon, your eyes fulfill this precious gift of physically seeing such wonders. Sharing moments of inspiration like these with your children, friends, and family will bring an awareness of all there is to see on this earth. What a treasure.

As you use your memories and all of your senses, may you refuse to stay in the shadows. Instead, turn your eyes toward the sun and go forward to lead a positive, productive life.

Joan enjoying the ambiance of Mt. Lemmon located in the
Santa Catalinas located behind their home.

Sense of Hearing

"If the whole body were an eye, where would the hearing be?"
— 1 Corinthians 12:17 (New International Version)

During my early employment at the school for the blind, a poignant experience happened that inspires me even today. Standing quietly at the entrance to the gym on our campus, I was watching three boys playing basketball. Like most gyms, it had the typical basketball hoop. But in our gym, a switch on the wall turned on clickers that were placed in and behind each backboard, giving each basket its own distinctive sound. The students did their best to put the ball through the hoop with great pleasure. Even the effort of throwing a ball in that direction benefited them physically as they used muscles that often get ignored. Making a basket was icing on the cake!

At one point in the three-man game I was watching, the ball slipped away from them and began silently rolling. As it snuck away from them, I feared they'd be at a loss trying to find it.

Also watching the boys play was my husband Joe. He quietly came up beside me and signaled me not to say anything. We saw the boys discussing the area each would be in charge of looking, mapping out parts of the gym in a grid. After several minutes of tedious, methodical searching on their hands and knees while they had ongoing communication about where they were, one of them finally found the ball. The trio immediately resumed playing their game.

Any frustration they might have experienced simply wasn't there! This turned into a profound lesson for my unknown future and my own patience. Now, when I'm coping with the smallest of tasks, I recall their way of communicating, working together, and using their sense of hearing to locate that ball in the gym.

℘

After I lost my sight, my other senses had to step up to the plate. Going through the relearning process, I experienced many "light bulb" moments. My first came when my nine-year-old daughter and I were shopping at a department store. Joy was my "eyes" using the technique of "sighted guide" by my holding her arm just above her elbow.

Looking for the escalator in this crowded store, we stopped for a moment. Joy was looking around with her sight to find it when I turned my head over my left shoulder and said, "Joy, I think it's over there." I could hear the motors that run the escalator.

She turned toward where I pointed and started leading me in that direction. Lo and behold, after a few zigs and zags, there it was! I had used my sense of hearing to "see" where we needed to go. Like the boys on the basketball court, we had worked together and it felt exciting. More important, I felt capable, and I felt relieved.

℘

As a speaker, I use my finely tuned sense of hearing all of the time and it has gotten me through difficult moments on stage. Here's one of them.

Joy, who was twelve at the time, accompanied me to a speech in Toronto. She'd learned to become an excellent assistant and instinctively knew my needs. The audience of approximately 2,000 people sat in a semi-circle in the theater-style auditorium. During my rehearsals, I had placed a piece of reflective tape in a specific area on the stage to use as a landmark of where to stand. This tape also prevents me from getting too close to the edge. Given the right lighting, I can actually glimpse the tape in my peripheral vision. I also requested that a stool with a back be placed in the center of the stage, providing another landmark. Touching the stool periodically and eyeing the tape on the floor keeps me in the right place.

At the time of the actual presentation, however, the spotlight was brighter than I'd prepared for during rehearsal. I couldn't see my tape! Consequently, during my presentation, I gradually turned and was only facing the audience to my left. Joy knew right away I was disoriented. So she cleared her throat and started coughing politely but consistently. Beforehand, we talked about her sitting in the center front seat. When I heard her cough and realized what she was doing, I slowly righted myself and found my landmarks so I could squarely face the audience. Back in business!

Giggling about this ingenious ploy later, Joy told me the lady sitting next to her had leaned over and offered her a cough drop. Joy nicely refused and her cough miraculously disappeared! (That a girl!)

Sense of Hearing in Our World

While deep in concentration, most likely you've had a moment when another person has come into the room. From the tempo of the walk or the sound of a deep sigh, you've sensed something was wrong. Your sensitivity, intuition, and reaction to what the person might need at that point can be powerful. Opening your senses to connect with that person and addressing whatever the problem might be can soften its edge, maybe even solve it.

All of this starts from an expanded sense of hearing.

In the business world, using excellent listening skills are as important, if not *more* important, than anything else. Paying close attention to everything we hear can make an ordinary moment more powerful. Expanding from there, understanding the vast interactions between different kinds of people—truly *hearing* what they say and finding out what they think—is essential for creating a world in which people work and live in harmony.

Insights into Your Sense of Hearing

Your life encompasses the sense of hearing in ways you often don't realize. In the world of motherhood, for example, you wake up in a split second when you hear your baby's peep in a room across the hallway. You bolt into the nursery to check in. Years later, you hear that front doorknob barely click when your teenager finally comes in after her first date.

Here's another example. While standing at the kitchen sink, perhaps you've heard your neighbor's car pull up in the driveway. Without looking out the window, your mind's eye creates a scene just from the sounds you hear. You hear the chatter of voices, the thud of a door closing, and the beep of the doors being locked. How do you strengthen this amazing sense? By consciously tuning in and using it to its fullest potential.

Your hearing fills your life with incredible information, both in the form of gifts and distractions. Even before you open your eyes, the sounds you hear—the birds singing, the radio clicking on, the coffee pot gurgling—start your engines running for the day. Those living in a busy city may hear wakening sounds that trigger the hustle and bustle of an exciting, busy life. These sounds throw them into a "taking care of business" mode.

But wherever you live, before you take off running, pause in quietude for just a while. Take time to sit quietly and simply listen. Slow down to experience that precious gift of renewal. Tune in to the whisper of your faith.

If it's not first thing in the morning, determine the quietest time in your day to close your eyes and be still. Whether you pray, meditate, or chill out, use this time to discover sounds you've never noticed before. Then allow other senses to come into your awareness.

I encourage you to use this sacred time routinely to replenish your body and your soul.

ᔭ

In our desert environment at certain times of the year, the brown-crested flycatcher is the first to sing in the morning. Its distinct, musical song has a beautiful rhythm. Before the sun peaks over the mountains, this bird seems to be gently awakening its sleeping friends and urging me to wake up, too.

Which alarm clocks of nature are found in your world? Do you listen for them when you wake up? Being surrounded by comforting sounds helps you calm your soul. The sound of water running over rocks, the sound of birds chirping, the range of sounds from your favorite singers also assist in handling life's stresses.

Have you ever dissected a piece of music from a full orchestra? Can you pick out different string instruments: violin, viola, cello, string base? Do you hear the oboe, clarinet, flute, and piccolo? Experiment and identify as many different sounds as possible. Follow the orchestra's arrangement and tune into the sound of just one instrument. Certainly, they're all important in completing the entire piece of music. Each single voice plays its role in the finished product. Can you hear it?

It takes practice to put your sense of hearing into motion and focus on its usefulness. Experiment. Stop to listen for the escalator's location in a store. (You'll find doing it easier than you expected!) Ask yourself these questions: *Are you a good listener for your friends and colleagues? Are you listening to sounds you have never heard before? Are you hearing the sounds of silence and the voice of God?*

As you close your eyes, essentially you're shutting out the world. But in fact, you should be allowing new senses in. In the upcoming chapters, you'll experience a multitude of senses. Use them all to their fullest potential, and you'll expand the joy you experience in life.

Sense of Touch

"Reach out and touch someone."
— AT&T

Shortly after my vision loss, we received an unexpected package in the mail from my parents who were living in a nearby state. Inside was a case that held ten cassettes. As I took out the first tape and put it into the player, my father's voice came through the speakers reading the beginning of Mathew 1:1. He had recorded the entire King James Version of the New Testament!

I was stunned. Picturing my dad at his desk turning the pages of the Bible and recording each word brought tears as I bowed my head to listen. I knew this was a gift of the heart, a truly extraordinary gesture. I also knew he felt helpless about my recent vision loss. This was the only thing he felt he could *do.* I was incredibly touched by the time and effort it took. Today, numerous updated recordings of the Bible are available. Actors of distinction have lent their voices to create beautiful versions of these words from ancient days. Still, my dad's treasured gift touches me as much today as it did when I opened that package in 1984.

I'm often asked, "What can one say at a time of loss?" My response? Using words is difficult and not always necessary. The most touching communication for me after Joe's death was often a lump-in-the-throat hug from a friend or loved one. The hug told me everything.

Mom and Dad at our reception held a
month after the wedding.

I also appreciated thoughtful cards, gifts, and flowers that arrived in abundance. Among the bouquets were sweet-smelling roses. One afternoon after everyone had gone, I sat alone in the quiet of the house trying to take in all that had happened. I sensed my life ticking away minute by minute with no real direction. Plus I felt exhausted and couldn't think much past the next task.

Kneeling down on the floor near a particularly fragrant bouquet of roses, I slowly reached out to touch them. One rose slipped into my hand. Pulling it out of the vase, I touched its velvet petals. What color was it? I didn't know and it didn't matter. Instead, I focused on what I was experiencing. The touch of its softness on my cheek gave a new meaning to "seeing" flowers. The fragrance filling the room gave me a sense of peace. The delicate movement of each petal and the strong stem with the thorn protecting it all became magnified far beyond its visual beauty.

So often we look past an important part of life, small though it may be, and miss the significance of the part it plays in creating the whole picture. As I touched that rose, I knew God would take care of me even though I didn't know where He would lead me. I simply had to let that go for the moment.

❦

Of all of the physical senses, touch may be the most endearing for me. When traveling to a speaking engagement, I'm always meeting new people. Most often, I travel alone and, without fail, it becomes an adventure! (You'll read about one of them—cart of misfits—in Sense of Belonging.)

The technique called sighted guide involves touching. As I take the right arm of the person helping me, I read the movements and body language of that individual. Now, I realize that the moment I take someone's arm, I'm immediately invading his or her personal space. Because most people haven't experienced walking with someone who is blind, I know I have to establish a line of communication to make my guide feel at ease having a stranger so close.

Using this sighted guide technique with those who have spent lots of time "traveling through space" with me is physically, psychologically, and emotionally comfortable. Each person has his or her own special touch. Having been my "eyes" since she was three, my daughter Joy simply falls into step. I'm in my comfort zone to the point of my not even thinking about what we are doing. My husband Jim has become so adept that I can feel his movements and pre-read if a curb is coming up or if we'll have to stop abruptly for an oncoming car.

Some of my friends have become used to moving through space with me, too. My precious shopping buddy Kim has an endearing gesture. While standing in line to pay for that special dress, she protects me from the hustle and bustle of the store by reaching over and touching my hand, the one that's holding her arm. It is a gentle, reassuring touch I'm not sure she even knows she's doing. Gestures like these squeeze my heart.

Clearly, the sense of touch isn't only physical; words and deeds contribute greatly to this multi-layered sense.

Moments of authenticity, empathy, and thoughtfulness among friends and family play a big part. So does what happens outside that circle.

My journey as a speaker includes many lessons learned from touching audience members with an information-filled handshake or hug. In a brief moment, I can tell when people came through the line to meet me with sincerity and when they would have preferred to just "walk on by." There's nothing worse than a limp, tiny grasp. On the other hand, a firm handshake accompanied with words from the heart rewards me as much as any gift with a bow. Understanding how fortunate I am to meet people instantly excites and fulfills me from the inside out. It's my favorite part of being a blind woman. And it's awesome to uniquely get to know people in genuine, touching ways.

When I leave on my speaking trips, Jim drives me to the airport and assists me in finding a skycap. There is always a commotion curbside for I'm busy with luggage, cane, glasses, ID, tip money, itinerary, and so on. Inevitably, Jim finds that perfect moment to stop me, reaches out to hug me, and calmly says, "Do it from the heart, Honey." Then he holds me tight and doesn't let go until he knows I've paid attention. For whatever reason, these now familiar words touch me every time. They slow the pace, put it all into perspective, and remind me of my purpose.

It's easy to get caught up in the chaos of busyness and fail to experience all there is to feel and notice. As I strive to stay in the moment focused on the goal at hand, only

then do I know I'm presenting to my audiences for the
right reason. At that point, I am able to hold *them* close—
and touch them with my words.

Sense of Touch in Our World

In some ways, our society has evolved to a place where
touching has become taboo. What a sad statement. We
know that for an infant, experiencing touch and affection
is essential for survival. During early development, human
contact nurtures and develops a trusting relationship.
Worldwide, many hospitals welcome volunteers to come
into their nurseries and hold premature and abandoned
infants as well as the babies of sick or addicted women.
This effort gives them love at a crucial time, providing
evidence that humans need the touch of others from day
one.

Occasionally, a young blind student who'd had little
nurturing would come into our school. The parents
simply didn't know how to raise a blind child. Some blind
children have been left to lie in their cribs for hours or sit
in a corner for days on end because their parents didn't
know what to do.

Thus, as staff, we worked especially hard to gain the
confidence of this new student. Our goal was to bring him
to a level of skill that was educable. For these students,
touching, holding, and teaching them to feel secure was
a slow but essential process. Once we broke down the
barriers of their unknown fears, they could continue

learning and growing into our limitless world of possibilities.

If we think about it, many people around us sit all alone huddled in a corner for days on end. This requires that we reach out, find those who are lonely, and touch them in whatever ways we can.

Insights into Your Sense of Touch

On the surface, using the sense of touch centers on physical nerve-endings. Possibly, however, the most effective experiences happen when you, through your words or deeds, touch an inner nerve and fill someone's emotions to the point of overflowing.

Have you ever hugged someone for a full sixty seconds? I give you this assignment. A minute seems like a long time when you count the ticks on your clock, but only a short time when you believe in the value of a hug. When it comes from the heart, the warmth of a hug combined with the sensation of security wrapped around it simply can't be described.

What else can you do? You could leave a precious, touching gift in the form of a recording for those you love, just as Dad did for me. On February 14, 1993—eight months after he married Jim and me—my father passed away. No, he can no longer hug me physically. But each time I pull out one of his cassette tapes and listen to his voice, I again feel the warmth and security of his arms around me.

As you journey through life, *you* can be that person who develops a wonderful sense of touch. Stroke a rose; hug your friend; communicate your feelings; allow your emotions to explode. When you do, you'll open your world to this essential sense. More important, you'll open yourself to be touched by others.

This loving but often misunderstood and overlooked sense fleshes out the picture of fulfillment. As you go about your day, don't shy away from gently touching someone's hand or even giving a hug. Find the balance of being appropriate and sincere. Then integrate this sense more fully into your day.

And as you lay your head on the pillow at night, know that you'll find yourself touched by contentment and love.

Sense of Smell and Taste

"In the progress of personality, first comes a declaration of independence, then recognition of interdependence."
— Henry Van Dyke

Looking for a book I wanted to share with a friend, I could remember its small size and approximately where I had put it on the bookshelf. Running my fingers along the row of book bindings, I came to its exact location.

Even though I could no longer see the precious book or the printed words on its pages, my mind's eye showed me what this old book looked like—its size and thickness. Removing the book from the shelf and then opening it, the sound of stiff crackling from the binding brought this moment to life. Its smell floated to my face and reminded me of a library, which in turn, instantly transported me back to my student aide job in college—returning books to the shelves. In a split second, nostalgic thoughts of the good old days flooded my mind.

It's said that smell is the sense most closely linked with memory. I agree. Because all in one brief moment,

that experience took me from thought to thought and —
presto — a memory from years gone by jumped into my
mind . . . all from the smell wafting from that book!

Similarly, when I smell the scent of freshly cut grass, I'm
transported back to being a young girl in California. The
scene has me standing at attention in my band uniform,
glockenspiel secured in its harness, waiting to march onto
the football field — a memory evoked because the grass was
always cut right before each game. I also remember walking
into our band practice room and smelling the instruments.
The brass, the resin, the pages of music, and even the music
stands played their parts in creating a special feeling. For
me, it represents the smell of teamwork, of everyone and
everything working interdependently to create a positive
experience for all.

Peanut butter and jelly, Bogie and Bacall, The Righteous
Brothers, Jesus and Christmas, the moon and the stars —
these (and many more pairings) simply belong together.
Similarly, both smell and taste bring their own qualities
to the table independently, but I focus on how they blend
interdependently. Combining these two senses makes
them an inherently natural team.

Think about when you have a cold and feel congested.
Food typically doesn't taste good, right? It's because your
sense of smell and your taste buds work together to give you
important information. As you walk into a home during
the holidays, for example, you experience the aroma of
pure heaven from the kitchen. You smell the food wafting
through the house, your taste buds tingle, and you *already*

know what kind of food is being prepared. Yes, combining these two senses is a natural act.

꼬

I like to compare how smell and taste work in tandem to how challenges affect your working with others. This doesn't mean these senses—or your team members—never work independently, but when they come together as a team, the results are impressive.

It reminds me of an insight I had early in my life as a blind woman. I was in an audience listening to my friend Tom Sullivan—a speaker, author, athlete, singer, composer, and more—who happens to be blind. On occasion, I feel that someone's words have been directed right to me, and this was one of those moments. Through Tom's inspiring words about the concept of interdependence, I began to understand how I could be proud of everything I could still do, although it would be different than when I was still sighted.

I found Tom's talk about using a guide dog particularly instructive. The amount of assistance these amazing animals give soars off the charts. Working with his dog, Tom described how he's achieved a level of independence that's both rewarding and exciting. His words that day helped me better *understand* and *accept* how important the concept of working interdependently needed to be in *my* life.

This concept especially hit home when Tom said, "Here's the bottom line. Life takes on far greater meaning and is a much more joyous experience if you embrace the concept of interdependence with your total being—heart, mind, body, and soul." Adhering to this concept meant truly using all of my senses to step forward productively as a blind woman. It also meant that if I tried to do it all on my own, I'd block my full capabilities for meeting the life goals I'd set. *This* became my catalyst to leading a positive and productive life.

℘

Some people can multitask with the best of them. They're often the ones doing things for others. But when it comes to accepting help for themselves, it's hard for them to realize they *must* accept help. And, yup, I was one of those people.

It wasn't long after my vision loss when I became hugely aware of the fact that I'd need help with many things I'd previously done independently. How could I possibly keep fifteen balls in the air at all times? I knew I *must* open up my understanding of when I needed help. Gone was the privilege of driving a car, which in itself took away much of my independence. At times, I admit, I allowed this harsh realization to get me down.

Today, I can independently do many more tasks than I ever thought I could. Asking for help continues to be one of the most difficult parts of my being a blind person. Knowing, however, that I *must* open up my understanding of when I need help has taken a huge load off my mind.

It's the little things that assist me in getting it right.

For example, at first it was hard for me to ask whoever was around if the can of soup I held was tomato or cream of mushroom. More than once, I'd wastefully opened the wrong one, and so I got more organized out of necessity. Today, I'm happy to report I rely on a device that reads the bar code on a can or package and a voice states the information in that code. It's amazing to use and actually quite fun. It's also an example of first needing to be *interdependent* for me to appreciate how independent I can be.

Eventually, I understood that my asking for help also helped others. In a reverse kind of way, those who assist me feel good about being there for me. Any feeling about burdening them slowly diminishes as long as I didn't take advantage of them. Let me say here that I'm eternally grateful for the never-ending kindness from those who have helped me over the years.

Sense of Smell and Taste Interdependently in Our World

Just as in the world of the visually impaired, the sighted world also functions on interdependence. An organization of people must meet, re-meet, and communicate often in order to stay on the same page. The mechanics of how a company works completely rely on everyone working together, thus making the organizational "machine" run smoothly.

This concept filters out into communities, states, and even countries helping each other when in need. As the assistance comes, so does the feeling of unity and a synchronicity that goes beyond understanding (as with smell and taste). It does, however, start with each individual reaching out and working with others.

Insights into Your Sense of Smell and Taste

Socializing while eating centers around the nine million taste buds that you have on your tongue. Many powerful business deals have been created over the table at a fine restaurant. The ice is often broken over a meal as you talk about foods you like, wines you enjoy, places you have eaten.

Where does smelling your favorite smell or tasting your favorite flavor take you? Do you allow yourself to take the time to transport your thoughts by paying close attention to these senses? What memories come up for you?

Combining the information received from partnering these senses can assist in creating a healthy life. Similarly, having mealtimes with the family enriches your daily experience and provides opportunities to connect with each other. And all *that* centers around flavors and smells. Who wants to miss even the tiniest moments of precious information they evoke?

How often does something stop you from achieving a goal because you insisted on doing it all yourself? Could it be you haven't correctly evaluated how to head toward that goal? Proceeding with the support and knowledge of your friends, your family, and your faith can carry you through it all. It's truly the lesson you must learn.

I know you'll find it freeing when you allow your heart to accept help when it's needed. Are you blocking the full potential of meeting your goals—personally, professionally, and spiritually—by thinking you can do it all on your own? When is the last time you asked someone to help you with a task you normally handle alone? Please know that accepting assistance from those around you can be the best way to meet your goals with efficiency.

Right now, open your hand, place it in front of you, and find someone to journey with you through your week. Allow that person to take your hand in return and, together, walk in a positive, productive direction toward what you want in life.

PART I

The Senses We Know

B. The Invisible Senses

Sixth Sense

"It's tough to make predictions, especially about the future."
— Yogi Berra

Following a speech in the Washington D.C. area, I was to catch a flight to New York, but a violent storm had rolled in and the airports had to close. I'd been waiting at the gate to board when the announcement came. Confusion and frustration filled the voices surrounding me. Thankfully, the airport employee assigned to me was terrific. She escorted me to the front of the airport where I had to stand in a long line of travelers to get a taxi that would take me to a hotel.

After an hour's wait standing in my business suit and heels, I felt pretty weary. It's important for me to stay alert and pay close attention, but when there's a lot of chaos around me, my stress can build and I'm easily distracted.

That stormy day, traffic was terrible and taxis less than plentiful. Finally, it was my turn and one of the attendants hailed the next cab for me. He put my luggage into the trunk and instructed the taxi driver which hotel to take me to. During the long wait, he'd been talking with me off and on, and he kindly assisted me into the back seat, telling me it would be about an eight-minute ride to my hotel. Knowing this was helpful. I like to be informed about where I am and how long a trip might take.

Sitting in the taxi's back seat, weary and drained, I cringed with every crashing sound of the storm around us. The rain made loud staccato noises on the roof and I could tell we were crawling along in a traffic jam. I leaned forward and asked the driver a question. He didn't respond. That was my first moment of feeling uncomfortable.

The radio was off, the windows rolled up, and the AC not on, making the humid closeness in the taxi stifling. I could hear horns honking, and our slow pace started to feel eerie.

I tried again asking the driver a question. I remember he snapped back with a short, one-word response. *This* is when my sixth sense kicked in. Right or wrong, I questioned if I was being driven to where I was supposed to go. The time had ticked by well past eight minutes. NOW the red flags in my stomach waved wildly and my mind played games with me.

To cope, I sat there and armored up. I lifted my chin and played the role of watching the scene outside of the car. Even though my nerves were raw, I calmly kept telling myself to look confident. (Well, maybe that was God talking to me.) Suddenly we made a right turn and stopped abruptly!

"We're here. Nine dollars," the driver mumbled.

He jumped out of the car, opened the trunk, and disposed of my suitcase—literally. I started digging in my purse for money to pay him. When he got back in, I gave him the bills and asked for a receipt. After he handed it to me, I opened the door. With my cane, I felt for the curb and promptly put my right foot into the puddle gutter. Water sloshed into my shoe. I stepped up onto the sidewalk and slanted forward into the thundering rain. I had no sooner shut the car door than he sped off . . . *fast!* (What a guy!)

The driver had thrown my suitcase somewhere and no bellman was around to help. I had no clue where to find the front door, plus I was getting drenched. The main thing I felt, though, was relief to be out of that taxi!

I continued to try calming down by saying, "If I combine my knowledge with my instincts and focus on the specific mobility skills that can assist me in an uncomfortable moment, I'll be alright."

Sweeping the sidewalk with my cane, I felt it suddenly hit the side of my suitcase. I grabbed the handle and lugged the bag to my side, then squared myself with the curb and reoriented my position. Juggling my purse, my sunglasses, my suitcase, and my cane—the rain still pouring down—I gingerly walked forward with one soaked shoe. What a fetching sight I must have been!

Tap, tap, tap. I discovered a wall not far away. I chose to go to the right and, about six feet in that direction, I found the hotel door. Thank you, Lord! A good guess or a sixth sense? Who knows.

I found a second door inside and to the left, then walked through it. I expected to find the hotel registration desk facing the front door, and I finally found it down the right wall. This felt similar to maneuvering the switchback lines at Disneyland but not nearly as fun.

It was eerily quiet in the lobby and no one came up to me or said anything. I began to wonder, "Am I actually in the hotel?"

"Hello? Hello?" I timidly called out, feeling weary to the bone.

Eventually a person walked out of the back office. I could sense he was startled to see me standing there looking oh-so-charming in the latest "wet look" and wrapped in apprehension. But he soon quelled my fears and got me registered, allowing me to finally catch my breath. With my chin held high, he assisted me to my room. After I shut the hotel room door behind me, I took a huge deep breath of relief. It didn't take long to find myself diminished to tears, my confident demeanor totally slipping away.

Nothing had *really* gone wrong, but for hours, I'd been tired, frustrated, and on guard. Mostly I experienced a sense of uncertainty. My sixth sense had not given me factual information, but the situation warranted my feeling of vulnerability. My mind took me to places that had predicted disaster. What I'd experienced, I realized, could cause undue anxiety for anyone traveling alone in unfamiliar surroundings and similar circumstances.

Today when I travel, I hire private car services. The

extra expense pays for peace of mind and the knowledge that I'm in the presence of an approved company. The driver knows ahead of time what I expect. Although this option isn't always possible for everyone, it was an important shift for me to make. I'm not sure how I could have changed the circumstances on that particular trip, but because of it, I've altered how I handle travel arrangements.

༄

Having a contingency plan is a must. So is living in awareness and being alert for anything. That's what I concluded after my dear friend Linda's sixth sense saved us from another perilous moment.

Linda was accompanying me to a conference in St. Louis where I was the featured speaker. After my presentation, we sat at a table in the main lobby selling my autobiography *More Than Meets the Eye* to audience participants. Linda was exchanging money while I talked with people and signed their books. We only had fifteen minutes to accomplish all this; then we had to hurry to our room, change clothes, and hustle to catch our flight home.

We'd had a particularly successful day selling my book. Linda was in charge of the money wallet as well as leading me around. As we expressed our excitement about the wonderful reception to my presentation and the successful morning of sales, we gathered our materials to go to our room. We crossed the expansive lobby to get to the glass elevator. After getting in, Linda pushed the button for our floor. But just before the doors closed, from out of nowhere, a young man stepped into the elevator.

Still jabbering away, adrenaline buzzing in my system, I didn't notice him. Linda, however, carefully watched the young man. He stepped directly over to the outward-facing window of the elevator and looked out into the atrium, making no eye contact with her at all. She noticed he never pushed a button. Perhaps because he wore jeans and a t-shirt unlike the majority of the hotel guests, Linda began having that funny feeling, sensing *something* wasn't right. She gently shifted the bag that contained the money to her other shoulder, placing it between the two of us. In the meantime, I was chatting away, *not* paying attention to what was going on around us. The second the doors opened, Linda swiftly swept me out of the elevator. Just as she heard the doors close, she looked over her shoulder. The young man stepped out, too! At that point, he looked directly at her with glaring eyes. Meanwhile, I was still busy chattering.

With my hand on her elbow, Linda headed us right for the atrium railing.

"Joan," she whispered.

"Yes?"

"We are about to be mugged."

At that moment, I could feel the blood wash from the top of my head to the bottom of my feet. My left hand squeezed her right arm tightly.

"What?" I said.

"That kid on the elevator is following us, and he is going to mug us, I just know it." Linda headed for the railing and planned to throw the moneybag to the open lobby below. She could see the young man following us slowly. Two cleaning carts in the hallway nearby provided a little activity and chatter from the cleaning staff. When he realized we weren't alone, he walked around the opposite side of the atrium and briskly headed down the hallway. Linda watched him as we walked back toward the elevator and got in. She pushed the button to go down. The "bad boy" kept throwing glances over his shoulder as he made a beeline for the stairwell. We both stood in the elevator trembling.

Linda gave me the play by play. Meanwhile, she clutched the moneybag close to her body and we both paced until the elevator doors opened. After landing back on the lobby floor, we walked quickly toward the conference area, totally on a mission. We were moving so fast, it looked like we were in the walking race at the Olympics! Then we found two of the meeting organizers who were willing to go up to the room with us and stand outside like guards.

Had Linda not listened to her sixth sense—had she not been alert and aware of what was happening around us—we could have been in real trouble. I simply had not been "in the moment"; I had to rely on her intuition. This kid had evidently seen Linda handling the money amid the hustle and bustle. He no doubt watched her put it in her purse. And to top it off, he saw she had to take care of someone who couldn't see. What an easy hit! One of the lessons learned was to be more discrete about dealing with money. Since then, I always request to have the book table *inside* the conference room away from the eyes of outsiders.

Thankfully, we ended up safe and much wiser from the experience. Yes, our knees rattled the whole trip home. Listening to those waving red flags, however, saved the day.

Sixth Sense in Our World

We hear wonderful stories of people worldwide applying their instincts and intuition to avoid a possible disaster. In New York City, the phrase "If you see something, say something" has proven to be effective. For example, in recent years, there was a newsworthy story of observant street vendors who sensed that something wasn't right with a car parked in Times Square. The bomb squad was called and their intuition and sixth sense had been right. The bomb was dismantled and their prudent, quick actions to contact the authorities potentially saved many lives.

Being aware and alert to out-of-the-ordinary movements around you can be highly effective. Don't think of neighborhood watch programs as a frivolous activity for nosey next-door neighbors like Gladys Kravitz in the show *Bewitched*. Today, having these community programs in place make a difference in preventing crime. You may just find yourself appreciating that alert person watching your driveway!

Insights into Your Sixth Sense

At one time or another, you've most likely said something like "It's just a feeling I have" or "Hmmm, I knew something was weird." A baby's basic instinct to explore the environment is called the kinesthetic sense and can be easily included as part of the sixth sense. This sense enables people to perceive extent, weight, or direction— with some having a stronger capability of doing this than others.

The kinesthetic sense has been described as "eyes" looking into your own body and reading what's going on around you. After my vision loss, I had to fine-tune this skill by doing the same assignments our blind students did. For example, walking down a classroom hall with a tapping sound bouncing off of the walls told them which doors were open and which were not. Practicing this made the skill like second nature because it focused on information that fed into the subconscious mind.

How much does your sixth sense play a part in your daily life? How important is your intuition in the interaction with those around you? Listening to your instincts is a critical part of living a healthy and safe life. Whenever you sense danger, make sure you're aware of your surroundings and conscious of your immediate space. You, too, are capable of using your kinesthetic senses—your intuition, your sixth sense, and all that the world is telling you—by tuning in. Make an effort to "see" what's going on around you.

Finding yourself preoccupied with your hectic life can result in uncomfortable and possibly dangerous experiences. In my experience with the taxi driver, I allowed misinformation during the cab ride to muddle the real cues; in the "bad boy" experience, I didn't tune in to the sounds indicating someone else had entered the elevator.

The act of being mindful can prove to be prudent, particularly in today's busy world. Keep track of those experiences that send waving red flags to your stomach. Do you know in the moment what you might do differently? It's wise to build contingency plans into your life, thus putting this sense in the proper perspective.

I encourage you to live in the world not looking to the future but having a strong awareness of each moment in the present. Doing so allows you to use all of your senses to their full capacity.

Sense of Humor

"The sense of humor is the oil of life's engine. Without it, the machinery creaks and groans."

— George S. Merriam

Because of my blindness, funny things just naturally happen. Being able to laugh at the myriad of comical moments has kept things in perspective for me. That's what a sense of humor is—a perspective on life that you and I enjoy.

During the early stages of my vision loss and before going into the hospital, I was asked to go to the Ophthalmology Department at the University of Iowa. After Joe and I sat in the waiting room for several hours, our nerves were raw with the fear of the unknown. Finally, the doctor assigned to me came to escort me into the examining room. I sat down in a chair that I could vaguely see. I was working hard at not stumbling or looking stupid. Still, tension filled the shadowy room.

After the young doctor got situated with his chair

directly in front of me, he said, "Now. Will you please begin reading the eye chart on the wall?"

I certainly knew what he was referring to, but I had no idea where it was. I only knew I was looking for that bold letter E at the top of a poster. Thinking back, I wish I'd turned on my "comedy channel" full force. ("Comedy channel" is a phrase coined by my good friend Mark Mayfield, pegged as the Corporate Comedian.) I would have begun reciting a litany of letters as though I were reading the entire chart. Or maybe I would have recited random verbiage as if I were reading a novel. "It was a dark and dreary night . . . ."

But instead I quipped, "What chart?"

The doctor stayed still for a long time. An eerie silence prevailed. Then he abruptly got up, scurried out of the room, and retrieved the head of the department! My nervous tension had created this moment of humor and, I realized, also rescued my emotions from going over the edge.

Even as I write this, I find that scene funny. Some say it's somewhat sad. If I could have seen the young doctor's face, I am sure his eyes grew bigger than ever when I asked, "What chart?"

ॐ

While stressful and tedious, the hospitalization that followed did include light moments due to my comedy channel. My experience with the Art Cart Lady is one of my favorites.

Several days into my stay at the hospital, I lay in my bed recovering from one of the many sessions of tests. Thinking about why my vision had disappeared so quickly, I heard squeaking wheels coming down the hall outside of my room. Suddenly the noisy wheels turned into the doorway and I heard a woman's cheery voice saying, "Art cart! Art cart! Hello. I have an art cart here. Would you like to change the picture on your wall?" Then she asked me about the different artists whose reprints she had in the cart.

"Monet? Van Gogh?"

Before that moment, I didn't even know I had pictures in my room. But I did know that shortly after being taken to my hospital room, the technicians put a sign on the wall behind my bed that said, boldly written, **BLIND PATIENT.** The sign was meant to assist medical staff going in and out of my room. So right in the middle of her list of artists, the Art Cart Lady stopped suddenly. She'd just seen the sign.

I knew it was my cue to speak up.

"Actually, I like the picture I have, thank you. You can just leave it where it is."

Then I began laughing hysterically, perhaps also because I was physically and emotionally drained. She apologized profusely and suddenly vanished. Later, I learned that the picture on my wall was a lovely field of wild flowers and it became a beautiful addition to the vision I held in my mind's eye. But at the time, it didn't matter to me whether it was a Van Gogh or Crayola piece.

Much like food in a buffet line, it all looked the same to me.

❧

I will forever cherish the sense of humor delivered by some students at the school for the blind. One of our boys in particular had a charming way of laughing at himself. (I'll name him Luke to protect the innocent.)

Like many children at the school, Luke had prosthetic eyes. As a child's head grows into adult size, the eye socket grows larger and the false eyes don't fit. It was Luke's turn to have new eyes fitted at the university hospital. The nurse from the school accompanied him to the appointment.

Walking into a large waiting room filled with people, she found a few empty chairs and showed Luke to one of them. Then she grabbed a magazine and sat down next to Luke. He found a magazine on the chair beside his so he picked it up, opened it, popped out his prosthetic eye, and ran it along the page. Then he proudly announced, "There, now I can see better."

The nurse looked over at Luke and then looked up at the people around them, their mouths agape. Mortified, she first scrambled to make Luke put the eye back in and then stopped and broke into laughter.

When they returned to campus, this "eyeball" story spread like wildfire. Even though it had been inappropriate behavior by Luke, the incident gave a lift to our little community. Luke definitely had his comedy channel tuned in.

꙳

When Jim and I became a couple, laughter proved to be the bond that has helped throughout our life together. Here's an example.

One day, Jim and I had gone to the grocery store with our long list of items to buy. When we got home, we were unloading the bags of food onto the kitchen counter: bread, milk, elbow macaroni, broccoli, butter, and more. Then I pulled out the M&Ms® to put in the candy dish. I walked over to the coffee table, tore off the corner of the bag, and poured the candy into the dish. But they didn't slide out of the bag as easily as they usually did. So I reached into the bag and discovered . . . elbow macaroni.

Jim, who was watching all this, piped up, "Leave them, Joan. People will come and they'll just say awww. Besides, everyone puts candy in a dish. Hardly anyone sets out elbow macaroni. We'll be unique."

Jim and I laughed for days about this and, yes, we did leave the macaroni in the dish. We used to go through several bags of candy in a month, but for some reason, the macaroni lasted longer. (Originally a joke, we still do this as an economic consideration.)

꙳

The everyday action of paying a sales clerk can be quite confusing for me. Some might even call handing over my credit card a slapstick comedy routine. Visualize this: As I extend my credit card to the clerk, she may not be quite ready to receive it. By the time she reaches out for it, I've retracted. This awkward back and forth dance continues until I say, "I'm sorry, I'm blind." One clerk responded with, "Oh! So you know sign language?!" (I can't *see* sign language!) So I laughingly said, "No. That was Helen. I'm Joan."

Joan with brothers Jon (left) and Bob (right) at a family wedding, 1998. The support of family has always meant so much.

I've had conversations with mannequins thinking they were store clerks—and embarrassing my nine-year-old daughter in the process. I have greeted people who were walking up to me saying hello. The only problem is, they were saying hello to the person *next* to me. Oh well. Just an easy way to make friends.

It's mysterious why certain people have a good sense of humor and others do not. Some use humor instinctually while others must work at bringing humor into their personality. When my family is all together, we often reminisce over funny childhood moments led by both Mom and Dad. I consider my instinctive sense of humor a gift from my family. The following incident is one example of many.

While visiting my mother in her later years, she and I planned to go out to dinner, so I pulled out a pair of brand new slacks, got dressed, and proudly put on my makeup. Ready to go. Then Mom, who was following me out the door, queried me in a matter-of-fact way.

"Joan?"

"Yes, Mom?"

"Did you want to wear that foot-long sticker on your pants that says LARGE?"

She reached down, ripped the sticker off my right rear leg with that zipping sound, and turned to walk out the door.

"Of course, I want the world to know I wear a size LARGE!"

Once we got into the car, we both laughed and laughed.

Mom always did have a glint in her eye. As a young girl, one of my chores was drying dishes while Mom washed them. One time I said, "Mom, there is still some egg on this plate." She turned and quickly replied, "What, you can't wipe around it?" (Just so you don't worry, I must tell you that Mom did wash the plate again.)

I could write for days about moments that touched my funny bone. A recent example came during a visit to our hometown when my childhood buddy Louise took me shopping at Target. At one point, Louise needed to pick up toothpaste so we stopped in the area, buzzing with shoppers. She rolled the cart up to the end of an aisle and said, "Okay, I need to run down this aisle and get some toothpaste. Because it's busy, just stay here. Don't touch anything." She knows I like to browse.

"Okay. Okay," I replied.

Standing there, I could see shadows in my peripheral vision that indicated some large print on the pyramid of boxes immediately to my right. I gingerly felt for the display and picked up a box similar in size to a pound of butter. Putting the box flush to my face and next to my right eye, I moved it slowly to identify what I was seeing. I had no idea if the box was black on white, purple on yellow, or some other combination, but the contrast did give me the capability of slowly piecing together the print. I could see a very large "200" printed on the box. I was just in the process of figuring out more when Louise came around the corner.

"Put that down! Put that down! Put that down!" she said, her volume increasing with each repetition.

I immediately tried to put the box back where it came

from without knocking down the pyramid display. Louise snapped my hands onto the grocery cart handle and whipped me off into the bowels of Target. I was considering suing her for whiplash until we finally stopped where no one was within earshot.

"Louise! What in the world are you doing? What was *that* all about?!"

"Joan," she scolded, "I told you not to touch anything! You were looking at a box of 200 condoms!"

"Well . . . I was just . . ."

"I know, I know. But to top it off, there were two junior high girls huddled nearby watching you!"

As Louise and I regained our composure and started moving toward the cash registers, suddenly we found ourselves laughing. I'm sure the checkout clerk thought we had a few bolts loose (and maybe we did)! Explaining what happened to anyone at that moment was futile. Just enjoying the moment and laughing with one another satisfied us completely.

Sense of Humor in Our World

It's difficult to find humor in so many of the incomprehensible events that make news broadcasts in our world today. However, even in the darkest moments, one can see how the light side can peek through emotional barriers and pull people through awful situations. For example, on the news, I heard two men sharing their story of scouring through the rubble left behind by a tornado. All of a sudden, they had backed into each other and bumped, butt to butt. In that moment, they laughed and laughed about it. In cases like this, laughter offers a defense mechanism that surfaces to protect us from the reality of what's actually happening.

Using humor in the workplace assists in creating both harmony and efficiency. We often identify the kind of people we work with by the type of humor and laughter they exhibit. Ever heard people say "he has a dry sense of humor" or "she has a nervous laugh" or "he has no sense of humor at all"? There must be an appropriate balance between serious effort and too much funny time, of course. But still, a sense of humor can be used effectively to bring staff members together—and even contribute to their productivity. Within my own speaking industry, it is imperative to allow audiences to laugh, even in the middle of important serious points being made. These light moments help keep participants engaged. I suggest this applies to people in *any* career.

Insights into Your Sense of Humor

Being able to laugh at yourself is an important part of accepting all that goes on in your life. The energy you receive from laughter has proven to be one of the most effective healing tools in medicine.

It's been said that laughing hard for five minutes every day will help keep you healthy. And, I'm told, it takes seventeen muscles to smile and more than 300 to frown. (My comedy channel begs me to ask "who figured that out?" If you thought your job was boring, how would you like to count muscles for a living?) But if this statistic is correct, it sure seems like a lot less work to be happy than sad.

Open your world to seeing what's happening around you with your own comedy channel turned on full blast. Seeing the "funny" in things can make for great entertainment. Why, for example, does my bank charge a fee for *insufficient* funds when it's obvious I don't have *sufficient* funds in my account to pay the fee?

Especially when you're having one of those difficult days, here's what you can do. Sit still, rifle through your brain, and find a thought, memory, or feeling that makes you smile. Notice the peace that comes from doing that. Or joke around with family members. Tease your children, laugh with them, and urge them to cultivate their own sense of humor. Light-hearted interactions with a child help instill a wonderful balance and lay the foundation for keeping things in perspective. Decide which people in your life make you laugh, then call them and request a laughter break. When I have those difficult days, my husband Jim taps into his inborn talent of quick wit and always gets me to visit my comedy channel so I can lighten up.

As you lay your head on the pillow each night, particularly on those most difficult of days, think of at least one thing that will turn the corners of your mouth up, not down. Remember those incidents that made you laugh;

they exist for a reason. So does this healing power in your soul that can bring you to a place of peace and love.

Your sense of humor—what a gift of calm and joy for making your life fuller than ever. Be sure to cherish it.

Nonsense

"A little nonsense now and then is relished by the wisest men!"
    — Roald Dahl as Willy Wonka in Charlie and the Chocolate Factory

Growing up, I witnessed my parents joking around with one another. It gave me the freedom to exhibit my own silliness and encouraged my sense of nonsense to emerge. Even today when we all get together, my brothers and many cousins fill a room with quick wit and laughter. Total nonsense is in abundance. I see nonsense as a buffer in the coping process—a good thing as long as nonsense and humor are balanced with other aspects of life.

Because of my nonsense personality trait, I've sought out friends who carried this DNA. My childhood friend Louise grew up in a Catholic home, and Dad, a Protestant minister in the Reform Church in the U.S., teased her endlessly about anything he could think of, including her religion. No one ever became offended.

From time to time, Louise casually went into Dad's office where he was studying, put her fingers in her glass of water, and sprinkled him in a priestly manner. Dad yelled, often in German, and chased her out—all in good fun.

One day, Louise again snuck into his office, her fingers dipping into the glass of water ready to anoint him. But this time, Dad was prepared. He heard her come in, opened the right drawer of his desk, and pulled out the biggest bright green water pistol you've ever seen! Louise ran out the front door throwing the glass of water into the air, Dad right on her heels. She was laughing and screaming at the top of her lungs, keeping a lead on Dad, who kept shooting a stream of water at her back. They ran in front of the church and all the way around the grounds. As the squeals of hysteria faded into the air, Mom and I rolled our eyes, shook our heads, and laughed at the nonsense. Today, perhaps, the police would have been called and Dad taken away in handcuffs. To us, this crazy nonsense was just *so* much healthy fun!

❧

My sense of humor has always come easily for me. I see nonsense as simply another level of humor, even "silliness." The fine-line difference between humor and nonsense is generally how people act out in situations. For example, nonsense includes physical comedy without words, just plain ol' nonsense. It might be called slapstick or even a form of tragedy (with humor defined as "tragedy plus time.") Comedian Mel Brooks has said, "Tragedy is when *I* get a paper cut; comedy is when *you* fall down a manhole."

I'm fortunate to have had my sight for thirty-two years. And I know that seeing the antics of comedians such as Jerry Lewis, Dick Van Dyke, Carol Burnett, and Lucille Ball molded a portion of my personality. Carol Burnett's reenactment of Scarlett from *Gone with the Wind* gliding down a curving staircase with a dress made of curtains and the curtain rod sticking out of her shoulders still creates hilarity in my mind. Without a word said in this scene, nonsense resulted. Her sidekick Harvey Korman couldn't contain his laughter, even though he knew the script and had practiced the routine. Carol's physical demeanor, timing, and attitude filled the scene with silliness—essential and powerful components to achieving this level of humor.

✿

One weekend during my early days of dating Jim, I flew from my home in Bakersfield to Tucson where Jim had been living for quite some time. I'd never been to Arizona and we filled the exciting weekend with sightseeing, lovely meals, and experiences involving butterflies. When I was packing to return, Jim came into my room and asked if I'd like to have a photo of him to keep on my dresser. I was touched and happy to accept it.

Joy, age eleven at the time, had been staying with Louise for the weekend. When I arrived back in Bakersfield, I had a million stories to tell them. While unpacking and chattering away, I found the framed photo of Jim so I handed it to Louise and Joy sitting on the bed.

"Here," I said. "Jim gave me a photo for my dresser." I kept unpacking and sharing my experiences.

Suddenly I heard them laugh hysterically.

"What's wrong?" I asked again and again, trying to pierce their laughter.

Finally, Louise caught her breath long enough to tell me Jim had given me a photo of himself wearing a monkey mask! I couldn't believe it.

When I called him to find out what it was all about, he explained that, years ago, he'd gone to a professional portrait studio and asked the photographer to take one shot of him with the mask. The photo even showed the photographer's logo in the corner! What a nut! At that moment, I knew. He was a man I could love being around.

Yes, the framed "monkey man" photo still sits on my dresser. I might also add that many of his friends think it's one of the best photos of him ever. Personally, I think it captures his true essence. I also think he looks sexy. But remember, I'm blind.

※

In my early years as an inspirational speaker, I took a trip to the East Coast for a daylong women's conference that featured ten women on the program. Up to this point in my life, I'd never attended a conference like this, much less been a speaker at one. I wasn't familiar with how it worked and felt nervous about all of the details. On top of that, I knew none of the people who would be there.

All of the speakers had been asked to meet in a certain room to receive the preliminary information the day before. I'd made arrangements with the meeting planners to assist me in getting where I needed to be. That part had all gone smoothly. That morning, I sat in the meeting room fragrant with coffee and donuts waiting for the others. One by one, the women speakers arrived, greeting each other with a squeal of delight at seeing their colleagues again.

I sat quietly listening, pasting a kind smile on my face. I had my nametag in place and my cane folded up under my chair. The other speakers wouldn't have known I was blind so if they glanced my way and nodded or said hello, I wasn't aware of it. I worried how a scene like this could lend itself to my looking "snobby" and thus presenting a negative first impression.

I could hear the ten women in attendance find their spots at the oval table so the organizational meeting could begin. As we went around the table, we each introduced ourselves and said a bit about our upcoming presentations. When my turn came, I did my part and gave them the "scoop" on my story. After that, I felt much more connected. As the meeting continued, my capability to fit in seemed to be happening. We were starting to bond as a group.

Lunchtime rolled around and I needed to ask someone to assist me. Fortunately, I had developed a rapport with a couple of women and felt comfortable enough to ask one of them if I could take her arm. We had all decided to walk two blocks down to the chosen restaurant, no problem. And with the gesturing of the two comediennes on the program, the laughter was already plentiful.

About to leave the hotel where we held our meeting, we made our way through the large lobby and were heading for the revolving front doors. Those in our group had walked ahead of me and the gal who was my guide. She was doing fine, although I sensed she was a little stiff and nervous. All the while, I could hear one of the humorists telling a funny story and sensed the whole gang was listening intently.

Then my guide led me into a section of the revolving doors. I was honestly trying to pay attention, but on the first go around, I just missed exiting where I was supposed to. In the meantime, everyone continued up the street except the woman assisting me. She just stood there speechless. There I was, going around and around in the revolving doors. Then she started screaming. The rest of the group turned around to see me alone walking around and around and around between the shiny glass windows. They came running back and yelled to me when it was the right time to step out. I could envision them standing there rocking and swinging their arms like little girls playing jump rope.

It was silly, but this revolving door episode broke the

ice for all of us. One woman even sat down on the curb to laugh off the moment.

Obviously, I could have gotten out of that turning door on my own, but knowing they were a little uptight about my blindness, I was happy to create a bit of silliness. I found my sense of humor and pulled them in with me. Because of this act of physical nonsense, they no longer worried about offending me nor felt ill at ease knowing what to do with me.

❦

When Jim and I married, Joy was still young. He couldn't have been a better father-figure for her, and I feel grateful to him for all he has done for us both.

From the very beginning of knowing us, Jim teased Joy about anything he could think of. Here's the first example. When he came to pick me up for our first lunch date, he walked into the house and I immediately introduced him to eleven-year-old Joy. She and her friend had planned on staying home alone for the few hours I'd be gone.

Jim reached out to shake Joy's hand and she responded in kind. As he shook her hand, though, she went to pull it away. He held on tight as he told her to let go. That got her giggling and he kept shaking her hand and holding on. This silly gesture quelled any worries about the man taking her mom to lunch.

As our lives molded together in those early years, Jim realized how conscientious Joy was about her schoolwork.

Even when he knew she had it done, he queried her about her finishing it. In response, she looked at him and said, "Yes, yes, yes, I have it done." To this day, even though Joy is a young adult, married, a mom, and working in the business world, Jim hops on the phone and, right in the middle of a conversation she and I are having, says, "Do you have your homework done?" This silly connection has always made Joy feel special.

Nonsense in Our World

There are times we can't help but tilt our heads and wonder how in the world our society allows things to happen. Imagine the stupid laws on the books that are filled with nonsense!

In California, an unmanned vehicle may not exceed the speed limit of 60 mph; in New York, the penalty for jumping off a building is death; in Texas, it's illegal to sell one's eye; in Nevada, you may not drive a camel on the highway. Huh? I don't know if these laws (commonly called stupid laws) remain on the books to this day, but wouldn't it be wise to have them (and many others) removed?

Regardless of your position on political issues, the amount of money that gets spent in our country, both personally and governmentally, is undoubtedly a concern. There are times we can't allow silliness and frivolities to prevail when serious decisions have to be made. As an example, educating ourselves and being informed is an important part of having the privilege of voting. Eliminating inappropriate nonsense in our world can only happen when we take that responsibility seriously. It's all about having a sense of balance.

Insights into Your Sense of Nonsense

TV commentator Andy Rooney once said, "I've learned that no matter how serious your life requires you to be, everyone needs a friend to act goofy with." And I'm blessed to have several buddies with whom I can let the nonsense flow.

Allowing yourself the freedom of being a little goofy can healthfully balance the stress in your life. Nonsense can lift the heart, touch the soul, heal the hurts, and bring joy into the darkest moments of life.

When is the last time you pulled out a water gun or got caught in a revolving door to make others laugh? Lighten up your busy life by spreading pearls of nonsense wherever you can.

Life presents tough times, but the balance that this sense gives can help you deal with the realities of living. As you weave in and out of your life experiences, being able to see the humor and nonsense in a moment can build within you. You may have to work at it, but it will be a job well loved.

First, make yourself aware of the possibility of seeing nonsense in a moment, then balance that silliness with good decisions for you and your loved ones. When life touches you on the light side, then make the moment downright funny.

Some don't come by it naturally; they have to nurture and cultivate nonsense. To do so, find a teasing point of exchange with another person that can be repeated, just as Jim does with Joy. It will tickle your funny bone and touch your life forever. Are you creating everlasting, cherished memories and special connections?

Right now, rate your own level of nonsense and decide to boost it a notch. You'll find that turning moments of your day into silly exchanges with those you feel safe with can be playful—and healing. Experience how wonderful it feels to end each day having lived a little nonsensical fun.

Sense of Reality

"Denial ain't just a river in Egypt."
— Mark Twain

After college, long before my vision loss, I faced new and exciting challenges in my first professional job. Working as a recreational therapist at a state mental hospital and women's correctional facility in South Dakota, I planned and scheduled leisure activities for my assigned clients. There, I commonly experienced patients who weren't living in the real world. Just getting through basic living skills in a timely manner was difficult for many of them.

One of my favorites was Lola, a forty-some-year-old woman who continually asked, "Are you my company? Are you my company?" I worked in her ward every day. Having been admitted to the hospital when she was only eighteen years old, she could barely get dressed without assistance. Her mental capabilities meant she wouldn't know when to laugh, joke, tease, or be in denial. Lola had no sense of reality.

Lola had grown up on a farm far out in the country. During all those years I worked with her, no one ever came to see her. Yet her obsession for wanting company to visit her was heart wrenching. Her records only stated that during Christmastime one year, the authorities were called to the family's farmhouse where they found her cowering in a corner. Nothing had been recorded about what had happened or what caused her breakdown. She was taken to this facility to live the remainder of her days.

My heart still breaks to imagine what she might have experienced. I don't recall her ever saying my name, but I grew to care about Lola very much. Eventually, when she wasn't otherwise scheduled, I arranged for her to accompany me during my whole day of classes. When I came to her ward, my jingling keys alerted her to my arrival and she came running with her arms in the air.

"Are you my company?! Are you my company?!"

"Yes, Lola. I'm your company," I always replied.

At that time, she was my assistant; today, she's a treasured friend from my past.

℘

Occasionally we meet, work with, or live with people who should be living on the "other side of those keys" as Lola did. In retrospect, as I thought through all of the challenges in my life, there were times I wondered how easily I could have slipped across that line and lost touch with reality. However, what saved me were my ever-present sense of humor, my family, friends, and that wonderful gift of faith I've been given.

Approximately two months after I lost my vision, my parents came from their home in Wisconsin where Dad was pastor at the church they'd grown up in. They came to help me out, although I know it was difficult for them to know what to do.

Traditionally, I have scheduled Friday afternoons for my weekly errands. On this particular Friday, Mom wanted to help by doing errands with me. So she and I got in the car and began checking off the list of errands: pick up the paychecks at work, go to the bank, do the grocery shopping, and so on.

In this beautiful small town of approximately 5,000 people, we had one main grocery store with lots of windows in front and a large parking lot. Mom, the designated driver (of course), found a prime parking spot right in the front row. Good job, Mom!

Getting out of the car, she and I hooked up with the "sighted guide" technique. Now, being the parent of a newly blind daughter, this was new for her, but after going in and out of the car a few times that day, we were handling it all pretty smoothly. So with my grocery list in hand, we entered the store.

Because of my hospitalization, I hadn't been out much, although I knew everyone in the community was aware of recent events and many had shown us their support. Still, during the initial transition time, Joe had taken over the shopping, errands, and endless tasks of running a family. When Mom and I appeared on the scene—she being a stranger and me the girl who'd just gone blind—I'm sure we were turning heads.

Mom and I cheerfully shopped every aisle, filling the grocery cart as we went. I held onto the handle while Mom steered off to one side from in front of the cart. For me, it felt great to be out taking care of things again.

After we checked out our groceries, I appropriately held onto Mom's arm at the elbow. Then we crossed in front of the car and walked down along the passenger side. Per my instruction, Mom put my hand near the car door handle and I "trailed" along the side until I felt the handle. During that time, Mom had walked around and opened the driver's door. We both sat down in the car and shut our doors at the same time. Then all of a sudden, Mom turned and said, "Joan! You're in the back seat!"

Sitting there with a bag of groceries in my lap, with both of us easily visible through the windows of the store, I could imagine all of Vinton, Iowa, watching us try to look like nothing was wrong. Was I about to cross that fine line of reality? A vision of me running around a mental facility yelling "Are you my company?!" flashed before my eyes.

I promptly said, "JUST DRIVE."

Immediately, the nervous tension exploded, and both Mom and I laughed hysterically as she chauffeured me out of the parking lot. All the way home, we laughed so hard we cried.

Again, being able to laugh about some of these difficult yet real moments can be healing and balancing. Okay, this wasn't a life or death issue, but it was kind of, well, embarrassing. My mother was doing the best she could without knowing the techniques. After all, she'd never had a blind daughter before. And I was focused on acting as normal as possible—whatever that means.

To this day, I have no idea if anyone in the store witnessed this "chauffeur" scene. I only know that the two of us needed the release of seeing the light side of a heavy circumstance. This incident allowed us to gain a measure of understanding and acceptance during a touchy instance of reality. In that moment, I was beginning to realize the truth of having no sight, while my mother was facing the truth of what had happened to her baby, even though I was a grown woman. And all that nervous laughter was laced with the challenge of accepting that I'd never see my own daughter's face again.

Many people find it easier to live in denial. I do believe denial can be a buffer that helps a person take things one step at a time. Looking back, I know now I didn't completely accept my vision loss for quite a few years. I've also come to believe a person can only handle so much at one time. Changing the image of "who I am" mentally, physically, and emotionally doesn't happen overnight.

Even to this day, I occasionally forget that I'm a blind woman.

But the reality is that I am.

Sense of Reality in Our World

On September 11, 2001, the world experienced moments in time that brought us to our knees. From the second we watched the tragic events of that date unfold, from the calls received from loved ones to changing our routines for that day, no one could quite grasp what life-changing shifts had taken place. The fear of the unknown permeated our entire world.

Eventually, facing the reality of what happened, where it happened, who it happened to, and who was responsible for these horrific events had to come into play before we could move forward. We had to acknowledge the reality of this day before healing and rebuilding could take place.

Recovering from tragic world events takes a *long* time. It seems that as soon as we start healing from one big event, then a tsunami or other disaster occurs and we have to start the recovery process all over again. Reality hits hard during these moments, but the longer we don't address what truly happened, the longer it takes to get on with becoming everything we know we can be.

Insights into Your Sense of Reality

Determination is an incredible catalyst for leading a positive, productive life. Facing the truth and embracing a sense of reality helps you create your own authenticity as you walk forward on your life's journey.

Try this: list major life events you've experienced and decide if they fall under the column of "difficult" or "easy." Now, pinpoint those events that seemed difficult at the time but insignificant today. Next, pinpoint any event or decision that once seemed unimportant but became one of the most powerful events or decisions in your life.

These dramatic moments make it possible for you to learn and grow. And with the free will given to you, you have the opportunity to make good choices. Telling the truth about what has brought you to this point has made you who and what you are. Perhaps you could even consider this a directive in being real with yourself.

The events that have taught me many life lessons allow me to stop sweating the small stuff. You, too, have treasured lessons that have helped develop your senses— and especially your sense of reality.

What jewels in life have made you face the reality of your situation? Do you see how critical moments can make you more tuned in to what you must accept? If you choose to look at these moments of reality as a gift, you'll head in the positive direction of accepting difficult turns and being more productive because of them. Conversely, if you don't tune in to precious moments of reality, you will stay bitter and perhaps never move forward. I guarantee you that your life will not be happy.

When I said "JUST DRIVE," I needed to move on

from that moment *right then.* As Mom and I rolled on through the parking lot, the laughter we shared helped us maneuver through our pent-up bundle of emotions. God gives us avenues to help us move on, but we must take the initiative to find them.

When you're dealing with significant change, you may need to take baby steps to figure it out. Time helps heal the surreal and what you believe to be unacceptable changes. Your first step is accepting the reality of what blocks you. When you do this, I encourage you to open your eyes to see the Grace of God and His wisdom in all of your life experiences.

Thinking about my "assistant" Lola, I don't know what happened to her nor do I know how long she lived. Given her psychological capabilities, the reality of her life wasn't normal. But I think being "her company" and providing activity around the hospital grounds gave her a sense of reality during that short time we were together.

Lola played an important part in my life, too. During moments of loneliness, despair, and frustration when I needed someone, she accompanied me and became "my company." Remembering Lola still makes me smile. God does work in mysterious ways.

Sense of Direction

"Following the sun we left the Old World."
— Christopher Columbus

I sat on the beautiful deck of Mary's Denver home—the breeze refreshing, the July sun comforting, the sounds of the hummingbirds on wing and a waterfall soothing. All this set the scene for a relaxing evening. Our hostess placed a plate on the table in front of me and said, "Joan, at three o'clock is the cocktail sauce and at nine are the shrimp."

I promptly stuck my fingers into the nine o'clock position and felt the cool sensation of the yummy sauce.

"Oh! Oh! No, no, I meant *three* o'clock for the shrimp . . ." Mary exclaimed, correcting herself.

I know she was trying hard to show both Jim and me she could give me directional assistance. But her sense of direction, or the lack thereof, are well-known among those who love and know Mary. Laughter filled the start of a lovely evening.

My friend for more than fifteen years, Mary LoVerde

is an author and speaker on life balance and connection. She's a dancer, a spokesperson, and to top it off, a beautiful sighted woman who admits to being directionally challenged. She has traveled the world, and I marvel each time I learn she has found herself safely home again. When she and I have attended conferences together, I make sure I stay close to Mary to assist her so she doesn't get lost. (What's wrong with this picture?)

"Mary, I think we were supposed to turn left from the elevator, not right."

"Oh, yes," Mary replies, then moves us into a graceful U turn.

In our occasional phone conversations, I'm aware that Mary is on the speaker phone in her car because I can hear the voice on her GPS giving her directions. Thank God for the technology gurus who have invented all of these new devices!

♫

Simply put, some people do, and some do not, have a sense of direction. And for Mary, not so much. For some reason, I have several dear friends who struggle with this important trait. Possibly I've come into their lives so they won't get lost.

For example, my friend Ann and I had attended a meeting in downtown Tucson, an area I'm not too familiar with. We had to park a couple of blocks away from the convention center and then take a few lefts and rights to get to the building we wanted. Since I didn't know where we were, I relied totally on Ann. At the end of the meeting around four o'clock in the afternoon, we got to her car and Ann said, "I'm not sure how to get out of here." (With all of the downtown one-way streets, it's not easy for anyone.)

We found the parking garage exit and inched onto the road. Concerned, Ann told me she was totally turned around. I asked her what street we were on but she couldn't find a sign nor could she tell me what direction we were heading. Sitting in the passenger seat, I could feel the warmth of the afternoon sun on my right cheek so I said, "Well, we MUST be going south. You should be crossing Broadway pretty soon, and then just turn left."

"How do you know?"

"Well, the sun is over there," I said, pointing to my right. "So that's west and we need to start heading east."

"Fine. I can't believe I'm having YOU direct ME," said the beautiful Ann with a tone of embarrassment. "If you tell anyone you had to tell me where to go . . . well, just don't." We both laughed. Pretty soon, she came across Broadway, turned left, and we were on our way home in no time.

❦

As a little girl, I loved looking at maps. Indeed, I was the official navigator for my parents on cross-country trips to visit our grandparents and family in Wisconsin. I often sat in the back seat, the map folded in my lap and a marker tracking our every turn. Instead of asking, "How much longer?" I remember announcing the number of miles to the next town. Understanding what's where and learning to read maps helped me enhance my already good sense of direction. Even without my sight, this sense of direction plays a part in feeling comfortable in my own skin. Especially when I'm in a new environment, I function better when I know which way is north, south, east, and west.

Knowing where I am puts me at ease and I feel at peace. After I married Jim and moved to Tucson, early on I struggled with learning the layout of the city. Thinking back to when I worked at the school for blind children, I remember the position I held for a while in the department that made tactile maps for students. Each item in every print book had to be transcribed so a blind student could participate in the classroom like any sighted child. The geography book maps were a challenge, but the staff creatively made them tactilely interesting for the students with all sorts of items: rickrack, buttons, string, sand, and so on. I knew a tactile map of Tucson most likely existed somewhere, but I wanted the information sooner than later so I decided to improvise.

One afternoon, I came out into the living room where Jim was sitting. I had a cup, saucer, yardstick, panty hose, and a few other odd items bundled in my arms. Jim looked up and saw my possessions, turned to me and said in a George Carlin voice, "So . . . you have your stuff?" I'm sure he thought I'd crossed that fine line of reality!

I proceeded to kneel down on the floor and lay out the items in a way I thought a particular area of Tucson was located relative to a bigger area. I explained to him what I needed clarified and where I was confused. I knew of one road that wasn't straight, so I thought the panty hose could be used for it. After figuring out what I was attempting, Jim slid down onto the floor and began placing the items where they belonged to identify their location. The cup represented a known building; the yardstick marked one of the main roads crossing town, and so on. Once we worked at it a while, I *finally* got a picture of the area's layout in my mind.

Every now and then, I walk out with my arms full of landmarks, and Jim knows we're in for another map layout and direction lesson.

Being driven around by others is simply what has to happen to get things done. I do, however, miss driving on my own. Whenever I get the chance, I love hopping behind the wheel. Don't worry; this only happens at Disneyland and on bumper cars. When Jim, Joy, and I were visiting Santa Cruz, California, we had to make a stop at the famous boardwalk—a place I'd gone many times as a young girl. My main request? To drive a bumper car.

Jim opted to stay on the sidelines while Joy and I lined up for the ride. With Joy's help, I stepped into my car, and then she went to find her own car. I was near the railing where Jim stood and he said he'd yell at me when it was time to turn to the left on the oval racetrack. I was all smiles as I wrapped my fingers around the steering wheel, hands at 10 o'clock and 2 o'clock. I pretended it was a Beemer, possibly a red roadster!

Soon the noisy sound of the electricity and the scraping of the cars started up. I was leaning forward just a bit, pedal to the metal, loving it all! Laughing out loud, I could hear Jim yelling above the sounds of laughter, the cars bumping, the sparks, and the motors: "NOW!! TURN NOW!"

I heard him and made a perfect U-turn to the left and headed down the straightaway. Grinning from ear to ear, I was in my glory driving again at last. I knew where I was, my sense of direction turned on full!

All of a sudden . . . CRASH! My car stopped. Abruptly! I'd hit the wall at the other end of the oval head on. Jim and I had forgotten I'd also need his direction there. Joy's protective instincts kicked in and she came zooming to my assistance. No injuries incurred, thank goodness, and I corrected my driving enough to continue the race. Jim still laughs at the memory of seeing me speeding—carefree and all smiles—directly into disaster!

꙰

An inspiring example of good direction for me came from one of my blind students. Before my vision loss, we lived in a fourplex that had two garages. We were in the ground floor unit while above us lived another employee. He had one of our students, Les, living with him as a foster child. This boy, in his teens, had always been blind.

One snowy Iowa afternoon, I looked out of our window

facing the driveway we shared. There was Les shoveling snow! Because the garage was set back from the road, the shoveling task was big. He started at the garage doors where he methodically directed his shovel from one side of the driveway to the other, moving snow just over the width of the blade on each pass. This job took a long time. I know; I periodically looked out the window to watch his progress. To say the least, I was impressed.

Another student that comes to mind is the lovely Judy. This young girl was about the same age as Les but had the worst sense of direction I have ever seen. She often got lost in her own dorm area. We had to make sure she was with the group when going for meals or we'd inevitably go back to the dorm to find her. Judy had no comprehension of this sense. However, this beautiful, willowy girl could tell you anything you wanted to know about the atom! She had a scientific mind and it puzzles me to this day how she could understand the abstract concepts of that world. *Her* good sense of direction was only in inner space. We worried about her skills for getting around, but we knew her intellect went far beyond the average person's.

Les, with the spatial skills to shovel that driveway, and Judy, always lost but having extraordinary scientific knowledge, each certainly had the potential to do well. When I lost my sight, this teacher became their student by inspiring me to pay attention to my capabilities and to go forward. I commonly thought, *If they can do it, so can I.* Les had figured out an effective process, found his sense of direction, and chipped away at getting the job done. Judy needed help from others to find her way, which was a perfect example of working with another interdependently.

Sense of Direction in Our World

Even when we are little children, we recognize rules and guidelines set for each environment to help us grow. Some are strict and some are loose, but directions exist for us so we know how to behave.

Possibly our society should go back to being as a child.

Somewhere along the line, proper guidance gets lost and people get misdirected. We see fear and disharmony in our communities and crumbling governments in our countries. Going back to the basics learned in childhood may be the direction that takes us to a better place of functioning.

What an amazing world this is with everyone coming from some place and going someplace else. Different laws and mores exist throughout the world. We as a society move freely about the world, knowing what's expected and accepted in different countries helps us understand how we must direct our behavior. Critical bits of information can give us a clear course in our daily tasks, depending on where we are in our lives. If only the "perfect ten" were followed worldwide, we would have a more loving, peaceful existence, thus more happiness and harmony in our society's direction.

Insights into Your Sense of Direction

The direction of your personal life may change periodically. You might change the course of your career, the location of where you live, the beliefs you hold, and many more aspects of who you are. Staying on target and moving in a positive, productive direction isn't always the easiest. Hurdles and roadblocks crop up unexpectedly. You lose focus. You don't plan. You falter in your strengths. What happens? Your sense of direction goes askew because of the chaos. Just when you think you're heading in the right direction, you forget to listen to the words that guide you. You find yourself crashing into a wall of despair, frustration, fear, and disappointment.

Isn't life just like that? Staying on task and remembering where you are is a lifelong job.

Are you struggling with your sense of direction? Are you finding the tools that assist you—whether it's a GPS, the sun, or someone coaching you around the curves of life? Tuning into the importance of this sense will help you to move forward more productively and efficiently. Thus, when you find yourself off-track in life, when you have accepted this realization, when all else fails . . . I encourage you to read the directions. In the midst of difficulties and times of feeling lost, take that deep breath and focus on where you're headed professionally, psychologically, physically, and emotionally.

Re-evaluating your life's direction will help you stay on course. And who knows what you'll discover on that ride!

Sense of Wonder

"If you enjoy living, it is not difficult to keep the sense of wonder."
— Ray Bradbury

During the summers of my college years, I worked as a waitress at a resort in northern Minnesota with other college students. We lived in rustic cabins and created wonderful memories of carefree adventures complete with learning and soul searching. We could use the facilities surrounding a beautiful lake, so one evening we planned a night trail ride, which led to one of my most incredible visual memories ever.

Crackling leather from the saddles and the clop-clop of the horses' steps created part of the experience that completed the picture for me. Shortly into the ride, with chatter and laughter filling the refreshing night air, off to my left I began seeing fingers of light reaching high into the sky.

Soon the sky became brighter and brighter. The undulating curtain of lights was mesmerizing. Someone finally explained they were the famous northern lights. I had never seen them before. What a spectacular sight of wonder! I'm fortunate to have experienced this unforgettable moment years before I lost my vision.

$\aleph$

The title song of Kenny Loggins's Christmas album *December, 1998*, takes me to a haunting place of wonder and mystery. It brings to my mind's eye a picture of fog sweeping over a cold land. The words speak of a boy looking out of the window and seeing a star. He is *wondering*. When I saw the northern lights, I felt that childlike emotion of wondering about it all.

It is not uncommon for music to take me to a place of wonder and conjure up a beautiful memory. The uplifting sense of wonder feels light and breezy. As I listen to Loggins's song, the memory of looking up at the stars out the back window of the family car also comes flooding into my mind's eye. Calm, comfort, and peace fill my heart.

I am often asked how I and a butterfly scientist—a man whose world is filled with nature, color, and beauty—can fit together. I can't see his tiny creatures, this is true, but the wonder of all I've learned from Jim's life passion has only broadened my understanding and heightened my senses to the world around me.

From my curiosity about his passion, Jim told me of his early fascination with the little "bugs," as he calls them. At the tender age of seven or eight, he stepped out the front door of his childhood home and saw his first glimpse of a butterfly. The black and purple Mourning

Cloak floated by right in front of him. He quietly watched it flap its wings as it landed on a nearby tree. That magical moment mesmerized him. So began his curious fascination with these tiny, elegant creatures that turned into a hobby gone wild.

When Jim and I were married, we moved to the desert where he had been living for almost fifteen years. The diversity of plants creates an environment for plentiful numbers of butterflies. In our yard is a plant called Senna, which attracts the butterfly species called Cloudless Sulphur. During specific seasons of the year, the plants get covered with caterpillars, and each of them eventually turns into a chrysalis. In nature's perfect time, there evolves a stunning bright yellow creature with a three-inch wingspan.

Jim had decided that Joy, his new young stepdaughter, might learn more about her new step dad if she could participate in gathering these "bugs." After school each day during the first fall of our lives together, Joy joined Jim in the backyard at the small, empty terrarium-like aquarium where he'd sequestered as many as five or six butterflies. Earlier in the day, they had emerged from their individual chrysalises and Jim would collect them before they took flight. By the time she returned from school, their wings had dried enough so she could be the one to release them. One by one, this eleven-year-old took a feather-light butterfly out of the aquarium, placed it on her finger, lifted it to the sky, and watched it fly away.

In the process of demonstrating his desire to bond with Joy, together they released about forty butterflies that fall. From that, I knew Jim would love having a child in his life and fully enjoy *her* youthful activities. But he knew that for this new relationship to work, *she* needed to know and learn who he was, too. I called it simply *wonder*ful.

Next came my turn. Often when a butterfly was barely out of its safe little home, wings slowly unfolding, Jim brought it to me and placed it on my finger. He lovingly explained the importance of the bug pushing fluid through its exoskeleton so its wings could dry. I could feel the miniscule feet on my finger as it slowly moved its wings up and down. I lifted it to my cheek and felt the delicate movement. Now, because of my curiosity and myriad of questions, Jim was including *me* in his world, too.

I asked Jim what the inside of the chrysalis consists of during the transition. He explained to me that it turns into a liquid mush. Listening to him describe what happens, I immediately felt how profound this was. The metamorphosis of the "bug" changing from a caterpillar into a butterfly is an awesome wonder of nature.

My thoughts moved to comparing this stage of the butterfly's life with a human's experience. I, too, had a time when I turned into mush during the trauma of going through all of my life changes. I couldn't think; my mind was blank of all thoughts and order.

We must all occasionally go through a similar transition while we are in the middle of difficult days. It is all part of the process of evolving into the person we are today. Jim's talent in being able to explain to me the different stages of the metamorphosis of his "bugs" connected us in a way that I could never have imagined—a fact of nature that's truly a miracle.

∾

Living in the Sonoran Desert, every day we sense a world filled with things to wonder about. Like the majestic saguaro cactus. I've never actually seen this cactus that can reach up to forty feet into the sky. I have, however, touched one. *Very carefully.*

The saguaro (pronounced suh-*wahr*-oh) is ribbed and has millions of spines on its outer rim. In my periphery when the light is dusky and dim, I can see the shadow of this giant multi-armed object. When I stand at its foot and look up, I can't help but wonder all that it's seen. A saguaro grows only one inch a year, which means thousands of these desert dwellers have been around for hundreds of years. Did they see the settlers coming into the valley? How did wagon trains ever get around all of them? It's fun to go back in time and wonder.

When Joy and I moved to Tucson, Jim had loaded his pickup with our things and we had headed across the desert from California, the three of us squished into the front seat, our dog across our laps. With ropes and tarps tying down our belongings in the back, we must have looked like the Beverly Hillbillies from the old television show.

It was early August and the summer monsoon rains had kicked in. As we turned east into Tucson and onto the road to our house, the afternoon sun broke through the rain. Suddenly both Jim and Joy took in a quick breath at the same time.

"Cool! Mom! There's a beautiful rainbow in the sky!" Joy shouted.

"It's full and hanging right over our home," Jim added.

In this wonderful moment, I couldn't help but feel God's promise to mankind and His welcoming hand touching our new home, our new life, and our new world of adventure with the butterfly man.

Sense of Wonder in Our World

When we reflect on all we see in our society that come from inventions, creative minds, and curious people, we can marvel at how far we've come. In the world of the visually impaired alone, the technology accessible to me as a blind woman in the twenty-first century boggles my mind. The creative powers of those who *wonder* if a new idea might work for someone who can't see is exciting.

Over history, inventors have added their creations to our world, enabling us to live with ease. Consider the invention of the wheel or the discovery of fire; they came from the sense of wonder, followed by experimentation. I can't help but wonder how Thomas Edison would react if he stood on a hill overlooking a city at night when the city below sparkled with lights, creating a visual wonderland! Wouldn't you love to watch his reaction?

Insights into Your Sense of Wonder

As a child, your sense of wonder may well be at its highest level. It's important to encourage children to find answers to whatever they wonder about. If you have young children in your life, allow them to re-educate you in their sense of wonder. Learn from their curiosity; it might open doors to discovering something you've left behind in your own childhood.

What do you wonder about? Whether it be the metamorphosis of a butterfly, the vision of diamonds in the snow, the marvel of the northern lights, or the lights blanketing your city, rediscovering your sense of wonder will *never* fail you. It's your path to hope and peace.

Let your questioning mind and curiosity of life drive you with the qualities of tenacity and purpose. Be the curious "animal" that touches anything, tastes anything, and investigates everything.

Have you allowed your sense of wonder to slowly dissolve and disappear over the years? Have you become jaded about the world around you? Have you let the experience of wonder pass on by? Do you think about things you'd like to see and do? If you've never seen the fabulous *aurora borealis*—the northern lights—start with that!

I'm well aware not everything we wonder about

centers around nature. But if you start there, answers will come. Don't just wonder about them and stop, though. Pursue finding answers. Exploring through your senses as you read these pages will lead you to a new appreciation for your life—perhaps even a "hobby gone wild."

Allow yourself to go back to your childlike thoughts and dreams, using a sense that you let escape for far too long. Open yourself to the *wonder*ful gifts of enjoying life and you'll activate your *own* sense of wonder.

PART II

The Senses We Need

A. The Senses of Choice

Sense of Belonging

"Giving connects two people, the giver and the receiver, and this connection gives birth to a new sense of belonging."
— John D. Rockefeller

Belonging is comforting, inspiring, and fulfilling. How do you incorporate this sense into your life?

Here's an example of a cherished experience of belonging that happened to me—what I call The Cart of Misfits. Now, I suppose this stereotypical label could be considered an insult to some, but whatever your abilities (or disabilities), no doubt you've had moments of not fitting in. These experiences have blessed me in my life, and I consider the term "misfit" endearing.

During the release of *More Than Meets the Eye*, the publisher flew me around the country on a ten-city book tour. I was most often on my own, which made parts of the experience somewhat surreal.

On one of the last legs of the tour, I arrived at Dallas/ Fort Worth International Airport. Typically, I rely on the airline employees to assist me in making connections from plane to plane. For those needing special assistance in airports, the electric cart is *the* mode of transportation. After I was escorted off the plane, the employee waiting for me took me right to one of these carts. She placed my hand on the back of the seat and I slid in on the last bench seat of three. At that point, I was the only passenger. She cheerfully told me she'd be right back.

A moment or two later, I heard a young woman's voice instructing a young man as they found their seats in front of me.

"Mark, now just scoot over and I'll sit right next to you," I heard her say. "After we get to ride on this fun cart, we'll go onto another plane, okay?" Her voice sounded kind, her phrasing slightly elementary. As they sat together, her arm probably around him, Mark began rocking and squealing with delight. I instantly related to the boy's behavior. I guessed Mark was about sixteen years old and the size of an average child his age. His excitement reminded me of several multi-impaired students I'd worked with at the school for the blind.

"Mark, now try to sit still so we don't bother the others," she said to him. That's when I leaned forward and said, "Hi. My name is Joan. Where are you going?" She told me she and her brother were heading to Phoenix and that Mark was so excited about flying.

As we talked briefly, the driver slid behind the wheel, and we motored down the busy concourse. We hadn't gone far when she stopped again. Very soon, another passenger stepped onto the cart and sat down next to me. Listening to him talk to the driver, I thought I recognized his voice. In a friendly way, he turned to me and said, "Hi! I'm Billy Barty!" His enthusiastic voice was full of life.

And I knew him! I remembered Billy from his L.A. children's TV program, plus I'd seen him in many movies, including *Foul Play* with Goldie Hawn. I guessed that he had his hand out so I stuck out my hand, too. I felt him place his "little people" (a phrase Billy is famous for creating) hand into mine. My huge palm surrounded his tiny fist.

"Oh my gosh, what a thrill, Billy!" I said. "My name is Joan and this is Mark and his sister."

Mark turned around, rocking with his arms flying, his sister's arm around him as she tried to settle him with a kind chuckle. About then, the cart quietly started up again. Billy chattered, "I'm on my way back to Hollywood. I was just at a Little People conference in Houston." His excitement was so infectious, I couldn't help but smile.

As we rolled along, the driver in a loud voice kept saying, "CART PLEASE. CART PLEASE" while traversing the congested concourse. I heard dozens of voices moving around us, and I pictured the airport with men and women darting from side to side pulling their roller bags, wheels clicking noisily and, for some, at a super fast clip.

Our cart had just started up again when one more passenger came out of the crowd. A man ran up to the driver and pleaded to jump on. He needed to catch a flight on the other side of the airport where we were headed. Explaining he had to make an important business meeting, he squeezed onto the seat next to Billy. I could hear him place what was most likely a briefcase at his feet. As he turned his head toward Billy, he exclaimed, "*You're* Billy Barty!"

Billy proudly replied, "Yes, I am."

The cart started up right away. We all shared a bit of information about ourselves. I told the group I was on a book tour, Mark was heading to Phoenix to visit family, and Billy had just finished a film with Mickey Rooney. "Don't know if it will get out there," he said, "but the film is in the can."

Meanwhile, the stunned businessman kept saying, "You're *really* Billy Barty!"

Billy was also concerned about making his flight, so he leaned forward to help the woman cart driver. Sitting on about an inch of the seat grabbing the back of the bench in front of us, this three-foot nine-inch giant yelled, "BEEP BEEP! BEEP BEEP!" as the driver announced, "CART PLEASE . . . CART PLEASE!" Mark was rocking and squealing, his arms flailing. His sister was laughing and, with my white cane sticking up, I was smiling from ear to ear. Add to that the businessman still in disbelief about sitting next to Billy Barty, and we created a powerful scene that was just a little hysterical.

As we hit a new corridor, the cart driver put the pedal to the metal. It seemed we were going so fast my hair was flying in the wind. Billy kept up his humorous beeping, Mark got even more excited with the increased pace, and we all laughed as we sped down the straightaway, driver included. (I'm guessing the businessman had a look of shock on his face.) When we rounded a corner to head down the next concourse, I couldn't help myself. I had to add the sound of squealing tires. This was fun!

Shortly after, we started to slow down so I could get dropped off first. Wrapped in smiles and laughter, I gathered my belongings and we all said good-bye. We'd only been together for, well, no more than ten minutes, but what an amazing blip in time.

For those ten minutes, we belonged together.

The woman cart driver escorted me to my check-in counter and asked if she could give me a hug. As I wrapped my arms around her, I realized she was of substantial size. Her voice filled with warmth, she told me she'd never forget this experience. We made a simple connection that reinforced the sense of belonging we both felt.

Reflecting on that moment, it was powerful for me to think that no matter who we are, no matter what we look like, or no matter what we do, we *can* fit in. I knew I'd never see these people again, but for that short time, we belonged to one another. I'm sure any traveler seeing our Cart of Misfits did a double take. But for six strangers during that brief encounter, we achieved a wonderful sense of belonging.

I believe building relationships is at the core of what keeps us grounded. Case in point: I belong to a Bunko group, a monthly gathering of twelve women. During this regular evening out, idea sharing and fun chatter about recent events (and much more) occur over the rolling of die and a score pad.

Because of our years of Bunko, these women have become a wonderful part of my social community. We've been "there" for each other during the good, the sad, and the mundane. If one doesn't have an answer to the question of who should be called for good carpet cleaning, the next will. When one needs help finding a house sitter, we feel good about assisting her. These eleven ladies, as well as others in my circle of friends, have become a source of support I cherish.

During the weeks I was writing this book, I had to really lean on those I "belong to." Here's why. One evening at home, I gracefully tripped over an ottoman and re-enacted the Dick Van Dyke fall at the beginning of his1960s TV show. In that fall, I broke my leg just above the ankle. It required surgery, a plate, and several screws.

To keep me going, Jim, Joy, and my son-in-law Brian changed their schedules and, with assistance from my Bunko circle, my needs got covered. Each of the women took a day to deliver food and support during times when Jim traveled. To this day, I'm not sure they fully understand how much their genuine acceptance of me means to me. I belong to them as "one of the girls."

My favorite quote from the movie *It's a Wonderful Life* says it all: "No one is poor who has friends." I'm an extremely rich woman.

Sense of Belonging in Our World

Repeatedly, we see people helping people, often through a deep desire and sense of wanting to belong. Joining service clubs enables networking, sharing, and exchanging information. These contacts provide us with growth and knowledge. The philanthropic service delivered by these groups is invaluable in keeping our society vibrant. How impressively these groups raise money and donate to the world of need.

International associations, companies, and groups create ways of growing and learning from one another. They beautifully enhance our knowledge of how the world is changing and allow us to feel part of it all.

Insights for Your Sense of Belonging

Like most people, you probably want and need to feel that you belong, even if you're a self-named loner. Through churches, teams, clubs, and organizations, you move to areas where you fit in and seek a level of comfort akin to crawling into your favorite chair.

Being a part of a family is an elementary foundation of life. Feeling the arms of the salvation of my faith wrapped around me within my family has provided a sense of belonging I wish for everyone. It's a journey that can fill you with comfort and love.

Belonging to any group involves duties, activities, and studies. A child's identity comes from an inner sense of belonging, thus building a sense of security for now and well into the future. When you turn your thoughts to the options of to what and whom you might want to belong, consider the beliefs and hobbies you already have. Which ones make you happy? Which new ones might appeal to you?

The sense of belonging, or *not* belonging, can flood your emotions when you least expect it. I've had many moments of feeling left out while sitting in the midst of hundreds of people. Whether in an airport or having dinner in a hotel dining room, isolation creeps in. How can I express it in words and do this feeling justice? Without the visual information of the exact movements around me, my imagination—assisted by other senses— takes over and creates a picture of what's going on. If I learn that whatever I thought was happening actually *wasn't*, that sense of *not* belonging becomes extremely real.

No doubt you have felt left out, too. Some people struggle with isolation more than others. If you find yourself feeling like you don't belong, just follow the signs on your personal map that lead you to where you fit in—like hopping on that Cart of Misfits.

In times when you reach out and remember to give,

you will inevitably receive. That incredible gift of belonging—to that person, that church, that group, that organization—will fill you with the joyful connection you seek.

Sense of Order

"Set all things in their own peculiar place,
And know that order is the greatest grace."
— John Dryden

During my early teens, in order to be confirmed and thus an official member of my church, we had to attend Saturday School—a half-day session for studying our catechism and Bible lessons. Eventually, we memorized the questions and answers, then we were queried by the consistory members of our church in front of the congregation. Reciting them at church was a big event!

During these classes, we usually took a break in the middle of the morning. Before restarting our lessons, we participated in something we called Bible races. It meant memorizing the books of the Bible *in the right order*. Picture this. Each one of us stood at our spot holding our Bibles upright in our hands with their spines on the table. If someone had peeked in the window, it might have looked like we were poised at the starting blocks. When the pastor (my dad) called out a Bible verse, we quickly searched for it and, when we found it, put a finger on the verse and raised our other hand as fast as possible. The first person to find the correct verse got a point. Then we read the verse as a group, discussed it, and continued with the game. At the end of the Saturday School year, the teen with the most points won a prize—something as simple as a pencil box or a bookmark with a Bible verse. The proud winner was always excited to receive it. Oh, for the simple pleasures of days gone by.

Decades later, during my boring sleepless nights in the hospital, I reminisced about many of my childhood experiences. As I lay there trying to pass the time, the memory of these Saturday classes was among my comforting thoughts. With a smile on my face, I silently repeated the books of the Bible in order. Having this precious knowledge in my mind helped me through the longest nights. In effect, putting my thoughts into an orderly place calmed the confusion and reality of all that was happening during those stressful days.

꙰

For a blind person, being organized is essential. I don't remember always being this way, and during my college years, I'm sure I found more exciting activities than putting things in order. My blindness, however, placed me into a world I'd never have thought possible and forced me to pay attention to order out of necessity.

Today, I'm proud to say my closet is in order. I can go directly to my long-sleeve blouses and summer dresses.

That way, I don't have to touch each hanger in my closet to find a particular item. In my kitchen, things are put in their exact places so that, with one short movement, I can go right to the garlic salt or to the milk in the refrigerator. Sure, I've had periods of disorder when I must start over and redo everything. But when I stay organized, the obstacles shrink and so do the frustrations.

℘

I strive to practice what I preach, but occasionally I get in a hurry, my thoughts are distracted, and I find myself in trouble. That's when I allow myself to revisit a specific moment in the cold of winter when, because of my disorderliness, I got lost in the snow. The memory of one frightening day—accompanied with the fear I felt—snaps me back into reality. Suddenly, I'm motivated to work harder at staying organized.

At the time, Joy was in first grade and, like other mothers, I was a volunteer in her classroom. The children read to me and since I couldn't help them with the words, they felt *they* had to help *me.* In a strange kind of way, Joy's teacher believed this reverse teaching aided those new little readers incredibly well. She loved it when I came in to help.

One of the days (about three years after my vision loss), my plan to go to Joy's classroom could have turned out disastrously. On this freezing Iowa winter day, the wind chill factor (I later learned because I hadn't checked myself) made the temperature equivalent to 70 below zero! We lived only a block and a half from Joy's school, and I had walked to it alone many times. Well before then, we had done the task analysis of how to get there, used the appropriate mobility training to lay out the path, and identified my landmarks along the way.

I *knew* where I was going on that cold, cloudless day at high noon. I'd go out the front door, turn right off the front porch, and turn left down the snow-covered sidewalk. When I got a certain distance, I would be in the middle of the street. At that point, I'd turn right, look for the shadow of the tree on the corner, turn left, and then head directly down to the school one block away.

But on this frigid-cold day, I was distracted, thinking of so many things that needed to be done. I dressed warmly, but as I walked, after making the last turn toward Joy's school, red flags started flapping in my stomach. Not feeling confident about my sense of direction, I slowed my pace. Because it was high noon, there were no shadows I could reference. The bitter cold created its own brand of silence while no sounds bounced off anything.

Confused, I didn't know my right from my left. Nervous thoughts began spinning throughout my being. I finally stopped walking, but I couldn't hear a car moving ANYWHERE. My heart pounded. I thought, *Once I lose my sense of direction, I may as well be in China!*

In that moment, for all I knew, the school building stood right in front of me. But I also knew if I continued walking, I might become more confused. Plus the cold at this dangerous level scared me and I could hear my heart pounding louder and louder.

Finally, I heard the tires of a car crackling on the snow-packed streets in the distance. I thought I was standing still in the middle of the road. All I could do was stand in place. Even though we lived in a seldom-traveled residential area, I knew the driver coming toward me would probably see me. Still, I felt nervous. I heard the car slow and cross in front of me. Then it stopped and I heard a window going down.

"JOAN! WHAT ARE YOU DOING OUT HERE?!"

The reprimanding voice came from one of my coworkers at the school for the blind. Just like that, she jumped out and came to my side. After she led me to her car's open passenger door, I slid into the warmth of the seat and melted into an emotional lump. All I could think of was *Thank God.* She wanted to drive me home, but I insisted on continuing with my schedule. After she drove me to the school and dropped me off, I strode into Joy's classroom as if nothing had happened.

But a lot had happened inside.

Because I thought I knew it all, I carelessly failed to take time to organize the task at hand. Even though I'd walked to the school often, I still needed to evaluate what might be different on that particular day. In this case, I had not made the necessary 90-degree angle when I turned onto the street. That meant I was heading south instead of east.

This perilous moment changed my life. My lack of staying tuned in, organized, and focused could have landed me in dangerous trouble. In fact, I acted irresponsibly when I think about how a disastrous result would have affected others. Yes, having a good sense of order is simply considerate.

Sense of Order in Our World

Henry Martyn Robert wrote *Robert's Rules of Order*, which became a widely used manual of parliamentary procedure and possibly remains the most common parliamentary authority in the U.S. today.

In 1876, while serving as a U.S. Army engineer, Robert was asked to preside over a meeting at a Baptist church — and did it poorly. Chaos controlled the event and Robert's embarrassment led him to find a way to avoid this kind of disorganization in the future. From the resulting actions of this one man came a universally used format that has brought order to millions of formal meetings worldwide. People turn to *Robert's Rules* for determining who speaks when, which topic comes next, how a group can work together to make decisions and resolve issues, and more.

Confusion, anger, misrepresentation, self-importance, and a lack of finding truth prevail in our society. Countries are being run by leaders who shoot from the hip. Because there continues to be a huge need for order in our society, many have developed other processes that work for their companies, associations, or groups.

Yet all order *starts* with the individual. From there, it trickles down into all aspects of society. When a sense of order is used, it's possible that we can eventually realize an orderly structure in our homes, communities, states, countries, and world.

Insights into Your Sense of Order

In looking at your own life, how organized are you? How orderly is your financial life? Are your personal effects in order? Would you be wise to find professional assistance or at least develop a sound financial plan to follow?

Some people are blessed with the skills to "work" the numbers. Suffice it to say, that's not my strong suit. If you're like me, accepting help with your finances is extremely important.

As you evaluate the sense of order in your life, be sure to review your documents periodically so *your* wishes are clear for the times when clarity is needed most. Updating your papers is like reviewing the steps you must take before going out into that frozen wintry day.

Before I lost my sight as a young woman, I could never have predicted the incredible changes that would befall me. Nor can you. Realizing your limitations and accepting up front the areas needing order and clarity will help you be organized enough to find the right assistance for getting your life affairs in order.

Amazingly, millions of well-organized people don't have a will, a trust, or any kind of insurance. Are you one of them? There is no need to fear doing what it takes to obtain such documents. You have the ability to do something economically and quickly. I commend to you the task of getting your will taken care of before your next birthday.

When Joe became ill with cancer, we revised our wills and reviewed our insurance policies. During a time of confusion, fatigue, stress, and loss, I believe having a will in place made me a better parent. In addition, knowing I'd have financial backing after Joe's death lifted a huge worry that helped me put order into my life. As a blind, disabled, single parent, *and* widow, this backing meant I could put a roof over my daughter's head. I cannot convey strongly enough what that meant to me at the time.

After Joy and I headed into our new life, I discovered more that needed to get organized. Although I didn't have millions, I required assistance managing our finances. I wasn't yet aware of how I'd make a living, but I wanted to make sure I'd do the right thing with what money I had. To continue pursuing my goal of living positively and productively, I turned to Stan, a financial advisor, who took time with me, reviewed my finances, and set up an orderly plan for my future. Because of this, combined with donations from Joy's grandparents, I was able to put my daughter through college *without* student loans.

Year after year, New Year's resolutions are made. Many people resolve to get organized, promising to start the year fresh by de-cluttering their lives. My friend Linda and I often tease each other about the difficulty of finding time to redo even one of our cluttered drawers, let alone our lives. But here's how to start.

Make a list of things you know you must redo, go through, or just get rid of. Start simply by taking one small task and making that a goal. You'll find it feels great to throw out the single mysterious and thus unusable key or the empty eye shadow case you'll never refill. Small tasks like these help bring you into a calm state, which allows you to see yourself as more efficient, more thoughtful, and thus more productive.

꙰

I've learned it's essential to give children a sense of order. When they know what's expected of them, they'll grow up to live more successfully. For example, having a consistent bedtime and expecting them to take responsibility within the family helps them understand order. Sure, they may fight the bedtime issue, but stick with it. Imposing consistency for them to get rest is the healthy and loving thing to do. In general, when your family experiences confusion and disorder, take a good look at what is causing the chaos. You'll likely find a lack of order lurking in the problem.

It's been said that a man on his deathbed never professes he wishes he'd spent more time at the office. Are you able to prioritize what's important in your life? Where are you spending your time?

When going through life changes and challenges, moving forward in a particular order is critical. If you can stay organized, you'll find the obstacles are fewer and smaller. As you prioritize and prepare for meeting your goals, slow down to evaluate every step you take. Keeping your head in the game will help eliminate the possibility of being lost in the snow . . . or lost in life.

And who knows? Maybe someday when you get your professional, personal, and spiritual life in order, you'll be winning the Bible races.

Joan and Joy enjoying one of Tucson's Not for Profit
fund raising receptions. 2010.

Common Sense

"Success is more a function of consistent common sense than it is of genius."

— An Wang

In my job at the mental hospital, another of my first assignments was caring for twenty-five middle-aged men in a locked ward. Although they weren't a danger to themselves or others, they didn't have the mental capability to come and go freely on the grounds so were considered "medium security." As a recreational therapist, I was charged with keeping their bodies active. One day, I headed for their ward on the second floor ready to lead the scheduled exercise class. As the door opened from the key-run elevator, I saw my favorite patient from the ward, Frank. He was standing close to the opening doors with his back to me. I immediately greeted him with a loud, bubbly, "Hello, Frank!"

That startled him. Frank whirled around and, in a flash, he slapped my face! Hard. Knowing Frank wasn't a dangerous man, I was stunned. Then the second he slapped me, his body slumped back into the nonaggressive stature he always carried. All this time, he never said a word. I knew he didn't even know what he'd done; he'd simply reacted to my voice coming out of nowhere.

I took Frank gently by the arm and led him to the office to report the incident. When I told the ward attendants what had happened, they almost didn't believe me, but the stinging red mark on my cheek provided ample evidence.

In discussing this later, we all knew I'd been the one who hadn't used my common sense. As a young woman just out of college, I hadn't *thought* about how I needed to enter a ward of psychotic mental patients. In this setting, greeting people with an enthusiastic, zestful voice could be disastrous . . . and almost was. Frank taught me a big lesson that day — to be more aware of my surroundings and get educated in what is and is not appropriate.

How often do you hear yourself say, "I just wasn't thinking"?

꙾

Common sense plays itself out from both sides: something you do yourself and something that happens to you. Here's an example.

As Joy stepped into her first professional job after college, she had her share of moments when common sense stood out humorously. Her position included working with companies served by her office. One early morning on her way to work, Joy decided to pick up donuts for four of the client offices she'd be marketing to. She walked into the near-empty donut shop and stepped up to the counter where a young gal stood ready to take her order.

"I would like four dozen glazed donuts, please," said Joy.

In the most sincere voice, the young clerk asked, "For here?"

Joy looked up from her purse where she was digging out her wallet. Then she looked at the girl and slowly glanced over her shoulder to verify she was the only customer in the shop. Her thoughts were muddled with responses to what this girl had just asked. *Did she think I looked hungry?! Or did she assume I'd have forty people joining me shortly?! Should I order a really big cup of coffee?!* This gal had shown the perfect example of no common sense.

"Ah, no," Joy finally answered seriously. "To go. And if you could put one dozen in each box—that would be four boxes to go—that would be great." Driving away, Joy called me to share this stunning exchange and the laughter that we couldn't stifle.

❦

Life places before us tiny but profound experiences that make us tilt our heads and wonder, "What was she thinking?!" or "That just doesn't make sense!" Like knowing you can turn right on a red light unless a sign says NO TURN ON RED. (I've learned this from the many drivers who chauffer me. Without fail, they all believe being able to turn right on red is common sense!)

I always wonder why the temperature in the doctor's

office is often cold. Sitting in waiting rooms, I've heard people shivering. And while sitting on the examining table, I have considered looking in a drawer for a blanket. I am, however, well aware that it's harder for germs to grow in a cold environment. But do I need to wear a gown that covers all parts of my body *except* the part I'm sitting on? Then I find myself sitting on the world's coldest metal table covered only with deli sandwich paper. I love my doctors and nurses, but it makes no sense for them to allow sick people to be cold at their clinics.

Since the loss of my sight, I've had to rely on my memory of how technical devices look, but how they work often confuses me. The layout of the number pad for both the telephone and the calculator could make more sense, in my opinion. Because the phone pad has a raised #5 key, using a telephone isn't really a problem. But when it comes to using a calculator, the numbers on the pad are reversed from the telephone pad. Have you noticed? The zero is in the lower left-hand corner not in the middle of the bottom row, and the #1 is directly above it. Common sense would have laid the numbers out in the same pattern as the phone. Thank goodness for talking calculators!

❦

I'm happy to be living in the world today with the amazing diversity and opportunities technology provides. The Americans with Disabilities Act of 1992 (ADA) has been a gift to so many. It's enabled those with disabilities to use the wonderful new inventions that people in the sighted world can. I am benefiting from this Act in many ways. I have been given training by specialists who teach the visually impaired and blind, thus I have learned about all of the updated talking technology. This has enabled me to run my own business and to continue writing. Other services have simply made life easier. For example, free access to the telephone directory service via phone is appreciated because I'm not able to read a phone book.

When the ADA was established, however, decisions were made that can only be labeled "thought provoking." For example, Braille was put on all ATM machines, including those at the drive-up teller. If I understand correctly, the idea is for the blind person to sit in the seat behind the driver. When the car pulls up to the panel, that person can reach out and use the ATM. However, a blind person cannot see what the words on the screen are telling or asking.

Actually, the Braille ATM has become a source of fun for people who realize why the setup doesn't work and they tease me about it. Today, increasingly more talking devices are being put into these machines. This is a perfect example of technology becoming more user-friendly.

Knowing that many people I interact with have never been around a blind person, I work hard at helping them feel comfortable when they're with me. I understand their nervousness; I had no previous experience in the sightless world before my job at the school for blind children. I do, however, occasionally have an experience thrown at me that makes no sense—as happened on a recent trip.

In most cases, the airline attendants are terrific and take care of me well. But every now and then, someone just isn't thinking. One time, an attendant came to the seat I'd been ushered to earlier and delivered the mantra of information about the plane and its exits. By now, I could recite it myself, but I do listen politely. In the middle of her running dialogue, another attendant, a young gal, grabbed my hand and, practically ripping my arm out of its socket, showed me the location of the light switch above my head. Guess what? I don't *need* a light switch. Generally, people mean no harm. But where's the common sense?

Really, it's more comfortable for all concerned if people ask me what I *will* and *will not* need help with.

Common Sense in Our World

Traveling on many occasions has allowed me to experience the differences in the mores and traditions of other cultures. I've found that what makes sense in other countries can be extremely different from what's accepted in America.

Here's an example. On our trip to Malaysia, the hostess assigned to Jim and me graciously assisted me during a shopping trip. While we were together, I felt a bracelet she was wearing and made the mistake of complimenting her on it. She immediately stopped, took the bracelet off, and proceeded to put it onto my wrist.

"No, no, no," I protested. "I didn't mean that I wanted it."

"I am happy for you to have it, Mrs. Brock," she replied in her beautiful broken English.

I soon learned that, in the Malaysian culture, if you compliment people on a possession, their tradition tells them it's something you are to be given. In their minds, it's simply common sense. Embarrassed, I had to let go of my belief and understand it was a "no brainer" for them to give away items like this bracelet.

So if you're traveling to Malaysia and other parts of the world, I encourage you to become aware of their customs beforehand. In this case, I told Jim I was glad he hadn't complimented any husbands on how lovely their wives were!

Insights into Your Common Sense

When is the last time you experienced a slap in the face that made you realize you weren't using your common sense? This can be more important than you'd ever considered. Even your safety can be compromised if you neglect to practice this important sense. So often, you're flying by the seat of your pants rather than paying attention in those taken-for-granted moments. You can suddenly find yourself in a situation in which your common sense could have saved the day.

A poignant example for me happened one day when I was rather young. I went over to the church with my dad who needed to check on something. I stepped into the pulpit and looked out at the pews. As I looked down at the stand where dad would place the Bible, I saw a plastic-covered index card lying there. The Lord's Prayer was neatly typed onto the card.

"Dad, why do you have this here?" I asked.

"Well, every time we recite the Lord's Prayer I read along. Even though I know it . . . it is easy to be distracted in my thoughts, and I do not want to misstate such an important prayer."

I assumed, particularly for my dad, that this was common sense, but it was a good lesson for me to know that even those things in our world we take for granted must often be refreshed in our minds.

Whatever happens, don't forget to laugh at the simple lack of common sense that shows up in your day-to-day life. I encourage you to look at what incidents make you shake your head and share them with friends and family. It will put you back into what *is* and *is not* reality. Finding this balance while enjoying these moments provides opportunities to complete the picture of your experience.

ᗡ

What can you do to sharpen your common sense and prevent disastrous outcomes? During the times you need to stay focused, you could refer to a "cheat sheet" rather than misstating a poignant message, or you could become educated in an upcoming event or destination to become aware of important related facts. Always keeping that ever-important sense of humor, understand that not everyone knows everything about everyone.

Also remember, what is common sense for *you* may not be the same for that person sitting next to you. Train yourself so that even the most mundane, repetitive parts of life can be more fulfilling when you consciously pause, follow along, and read the words you know so well.

It's highly possible the biggest successes in your life will come through sharpening your common sense.

Sense of Honor

"Honor thy mother and thy father, that thy days may be long upon the land which the Lord thy God giveth thee."
— Deuteronomy 5:16

A comment from a teacher, a thoughtful gift from a friend, an award from your company, or even a gesture of recognition from a parent on a job well done. These can all produce treasured moments of feeling honored.

One of the most special honors I've ever experienced couldn't have taken longer than five minutes. One Sunday afternoon after Joy and I had moved back to Bakersfield during our rebuilding years, my father and I were alone in the living room—Dad in his recliner and me comfortably on the couch. In his strong German brogue, he said, "I read your book."

"You did?" I was stunned. I became more than a little nervous.

"Yup." He paused and I waited. "I can't believe all of the details you remembered."

I wondered if he was looking at me. Even though I

couldn't look into his eyes, I ached with caring about what he thought.

"I know, Dad," I said. "I just had to write it down. So much had happened, and it felt good to get it out of my head and onto paper."

"Well," he said calmly, "I'm proud of you."

Whoa.

My brothers and I didn't grow up in a demonstrative family so this was a big moment for me and out of character for him. Even years later, I'm touched when I relive that brief, poignant moment when Dad's words encouraged me, humbled me, and honored me.

For the previous two years, I had been writing down my life experiences. Just a few days before this conversation with Dad, I had given a very, very rough piece of my writing to Mom to read. Within four hours, she'd read what would eventually become my published autobiography, *More Than Meets the Eye*. She had called me over to discuss what I had recorded in those many pages. That in itself was a big deal. At the time, I didn't know Mom had passed my journal on to Dad, much less that he'd read it.

Sadly, Dad did not live to see *More Than Meets the Eye* published. But knowing he took the time to read my journal and had the desire to tell me how he felt about it was powerful. Yes, the conversation was short. All of a sudden, the subject safely switched to talk about the Cubs baseball game on television. The sense of honor he gave me, though—that tiny moment in time—will encourage me and reside in my heart forever.

This conversation also demonstrated to me that, no matter our age, our words carry a lot of weight with our children. The smallest of moments get tucked away in a child's mind, only becoming defined once they are adults. I believe it is an honor for God to choose us to do the job of parenting. We must take it seriously.

꩜

As an inspirational speaker, one can be in situations sitting next to or talking with extraordinarily interesting people. Some of my colleagues have been honored to speak at the White House. They've traveled the world with renowned figures and opened for big-time celebrities. It's always fun to hear about the experiences they've lived.

One powerful moment for me happened in my hometown of Bakersfield, California. The Borton, Petrini, and Conron law firm had been hosting a business conference for many years—a prestigious one that had won many national awards. The exciting event was always held under possibly the largest tent ever made, housing as many as 12,000 attendees. Conference sessions went all day and into the evening. Over the years, the organizers had to limit that huge number of attendees or the event would have grown even larger.

In 1998, I was asked to speak in the business tent at this conference—a venue that seats around 1,000 people.

I was honored to even be considered, much less asked to speak. I was part of the lineup of well-known politicians that included John Major, former British Prime Minister, Bob and Elizabeth Dole (instrumental in U.S. politics at the time), and Shimon Peres, former Prime Minister and President of Israel.

Jim and I were given a hotel room and the limo picked us up from there the morning of the conference. My mother and my buddy Louise joined us to ride along. We planned to meet my brother Jon and his wife Kala on the grounds. As we rode in a limo *in our own hometown*, the surreal feeling of what we were a part of was only surpassed by our actual experiences.

Joan with Benazir Bhutto at the Bakersfield
Business Conference. Extraordinary! 1998

Pulling into the grounds at the Cal State Bakersfield campus, our limo driver had to move over to let another limo pass. As usual, Jim was announcing the play by play to me, describing the bumpers of the limo displaying small American flags rippling in the breeze. As we pulled to a stop, the driver got out to open our door. Mom and Louise slid out first, then Jim. I could hear lots of voices. My turn next. I slid along the rich leather putting one foot down and then the other as I stepped out to hear, "Good morning, good morning, good morning."

A deep, strongly accented voice greeted each of us. Slowly and distinctly, he took each of our hands and regally welcomed us to our day. Henry Kissinger, secretary of state for former President Richard Nixon, was the conference's first official voice we heard!

I was honored yet humbled by the fact that Kissinger was *our* welcoming committee. We just went with it.

In the backstage area was a buffet for speakers and their guests to eat at any time. After I'd finished the first of my two talks, Jim fixed me a plate and we found a table for four. Soon a woman and her associate asked if they could join us—former Prime Minister Benazir Bhutto of Pakistan. Really! There we were, "doing lunch" with this incredible world leader who had experienced imprisonment, exile, and danger as she fought for social justice in her country. Afterward, she and I—two women from different ends of the earth and very different faiths—sat together on the couch in the green room and we talked at length. Occasionally, she'd ask me what to do next regarding the meeting schedule. The conference was running just a little behind and she was concerned about meeting with someone. I reassured her the organizers would come get her when it was time to speak to her audience of 12,000. Imagine! This woman who (I was told) sat with perfect posture, looking beautiful in her flowing, colorful silks, prayer beads in hand, was asking *my* advice. I know we didn't have a world-altering conversation, but I still felt extremely honored to have met Prime Minister Bhutto.

Over the years, we followed Benazir's life via write-ups in the paper or comments on the TV news. Hearing about her assassination in 2007, I felt terribly saddened. No, we didn't become friends, but I'll always remember how she had honored me as we chatted on that afternoon.

⟡

Living in Tucson, I have been fortunate to have the opportunity to speak once a month at the world-renowned Canyon Ranch Health Spa and Resort. Guests at the Ranch receive a list of activities and lectures, and my evening talk is just one of their many options. My dear friend Jill most often accompanies me to these talks.

One evening in March, 1998, the group gathered to hear me numbered around forty-five. Held in a classroom setting, this talk is more casual than most of my professional presentations. At the end of it, we have an open discussion and time to answer questions. The Q and A period gives me the opportunity to learn about my audience members and where their thoughts have gone.

To get the ball rolling, I ask where each person hails from. On this spring evening, a woman on my left spoke up and said, "I'm from Chicago!"

"Oh great! Go Cubs!" I said. "My parents grew up in Wisconsin. My father was a die-hard Cubs fan even before he was born. That dictated us all becoming Cubs fans in our family!"

Soon the time was up and I graciously thanked everyone for coming. Usually everyone heads out the door for their last massage or facial of the day. As Jill came to assist me, though, I sensed that the guests were lingering for an unusually long time. Suddenly two hands turned my shoulders to face him and I heard, "Joan, I'm Ernie Banks." My mouth dropped and my hands came to my face. "I can't believe it!" His wife Liz patted me on the shoulder saying, "You're meeting Ernie Banks! You're meeting Ernie Banks!"

A pro baseball Hall of Fame member, Ernie is famously known as Mr. Cub. He played as a shortstop and first baseman for the Chicago Cubs from 1953 through 1971. In my mind, I saw my father sitting in the faded green barrel lawn chair in our front yard. In the summers, he'd be holding a small transistor radio to his ear so he could tune in the nearest Cubs game. Ernie Banks was one of his favorite players. I was humbled to know Mr. Cub had sat there for an hour listening to *my* story.

As Ernie and I talked, the rest of the guests stood watching, knowing I wasn't aware he'd been present. When I'd mentioned the Cubs, they knew Ernie would want to talk to me—and they curiously wanted to see what would happen.

Before we parted, Ernie asked, "Could you and the Butterfly Man come to lunch with us?"

I knew Jim wouldn't believe this one! But two days later, Jim and I came to the Ranch and ate lunch with Liz and Ernie. Now, Jim's enthusiasm for baseball is surpassed only by his knowledge of the world of butterflies, so this was exciting!

Our luncheon conversation began easily.

"Jim?" Ernie asked with his voice directly pointed at Jim, "How are butterflies like people?"

Ernie and Liz Banks with Joan and Jim after
an exciting luncheon! 1998

Wow. What a question!

But with only a short pause, Jim replied, "Well, Ernie, I guess we are all survivors." Jim hadn't skipped a beat. "The butterfly lays her eggs, sometimes a hundred at a time. Often because of predators and nature, and because they are at the bottom of the food chain, only ONE of that hundred may survive."

He held Ernie and Liz spellbound by the realization of how difficult nature can be. All of a sudden, Jim reached into his shirt pocket and pulled out a small vial. In it was a caterpillar. Yikes! Jim had come prepared with items for show and tell, and now I was nervous. I never know what to expect with him.

Jim gently laid the critter onto the table and Liz squealed, "What is that?!"

"Well, it's a caterpillar," Jim said smiling through his words. "Doesn't it look like a bird dropping? It's the caterpillar of a Red-spotted Purple and the disguise is for protection from predators."

Ernie was leaning forward, studying the creature with amazement, and Liz was verbalizing soft sounds of disgust. Our waiter walked up to begin the service and came to an abrupt halt.

"Oh, my gosh!" the waiter sputtered nervously as he pulled out a napkin. "What is that?! I am SO sorry! Was that on the table?! Here! Let me get that for you!"

We all laughed. Jim stopped the waiter, lifted the little critter off the table, and put it back into the vial and then his pocket. Only Jim Brock would go to lunch at a health spa with "bugs" as his guest.

During our conversation, Liz and Ernie asked question after question, listening intently throughout the delicious meal. Ernie's wheels were turning as he wondered how inner city children might benefit by learning about this beautiful part of nature. The discussion evolved into how we all go through tough life moments and have to survive. Some don't make it through, just like the tiny eggs of the butterfly. Then Ernie shared that for two years after his retirement from baseball, he'd experienced bad dreams. He'd never won a World Series, thus he'd never worn a World Series ring. We could tell the great sadness in his heart, but he had survived that. And I know he's been honored by many recognitions and the love of his fans. Yes, we are *all* survivors, just as Jim had said.

I felt proud to be there, just as if we had lunch with Ernie and his lovely wife every day. But I also felt honored even more because, as Jim's wife, I was a part of the Butterfly Man. This gentle, funny, shy guy was again touching lives through his "hobby gone wild."

By the way, during our two-hour lunch, Jim did get in about fifteen minutes of baseball questions. I know my father would have been thrilled to sit there, too, but I think Dad would have been even happier to know that Ernie was the humble, kind man he'd always imagined him to be. We will always treasure the memory of this extraordinary moment.

Sense of Honor in Our World

We often have activities that honor those among us. We honor those who have served and protected us; we pause in silence to honor those who have fallen; we stand to salute the American flag. Companies and associations honor the employee who has achieved a level of accomplishment beyond the norm. This recognition boosts morale within an organization, providing encouragement and support.

We know that honoring others uplifts their spirits with a much-needed pat on the back and builds a sense of honor that has great value in our world.

Insights into Your Sense of Honor

Your own experiences of being honored don't require big names, world-changing accomplishments, or life-altering events. But when you simply ponder awhile and tap into incidents from your own experiences, understanding how to view your sense of honor will bless you.

I can't help but believe *everyone* wants to be honorable and respectful. Examine how others have honored you, just as my father honored me when he acknowledged reading my book. You will find the jewels of honor in moments you least expect. So accept the compliments that come to you and study what was meant by them. Allow yourself to feel pride as well as honor in what you've created.

An important part of the sense of honor is being able to reciprocate. When is the last time you praised someone of significance in your life? Saluting a person you know is as rewarding as receiving the honor yourself. What you learn from those moments becomes a gift that fills your heart with joy. You can only be thrilled for that person!

Honoring your parents is a directive given by God. The little child wants only to please a parent and always craves the pats on the back. Even as an adult, you remain a child to that parent. The words of love and support that come from your parent can honor you forever. *This simply never changes.*

Indeed, knowing how it made you feel when you were praised or shown love by your parent sets the example of how all children in your life want to be treated. And keeping this at the surface of your thoughts helps secure the positive relationships you're reaching for in the world of parenting.

It's said that you can know someone by the friends they keep and how they treat those friends. Ernie Banks celebrates his celebrity with pride and honor. When he walked into the dining room that day to have lunch with us, he stopped and talked with each and every person who greeted him. It was evident he felt honored by their kindness and he showed genuine interest in them in return.

Surrounding yourself with good people—those who honor your life—is the right thing to do. Be assured that you will be blessed by the actions you take and the way you live when you embrace your own sense of honor.

Sense of Responsibility

"The price of greatness is responsibility."
                               – Sir Winston Churchill

Each summer for a number of years, our church joined with the members of a nearby sister congregation for a few days at a camp on Greenhorn Mountain outside of Bakersfield.

Camp Yenis Hante, a vaguely Native American made-up name like those given to summer camps, is a beautifully pine-filled area that's still there in Kern County, California. What a wonderful time for a kid! We spent many happy days in fellowship, hiking, playing sports, and just being together.

A favorite memory for me is the bonfire after the evening services. I can remember the men in the church working hard to ensure the fire was completely out as the campers returned to their cabins. Because of the importance of this task, they showed a strong sense of responsibility to do it well.

One rule of the camp I have never forgotten is this:

at the end of the week, we had to leave the camp better than we found it. No matter how clean or well organized it was at the beginning, we had to make it better for the next group at the end. Sometimes it was only an extra scrubbing of the dining room, improving a path, or repairing a stone step, but there was always something we could do. What an incredible example of mirroring the sense of responsibility for the children who came.

In my world as a "disabled" person, I find myself striving hard to achieve things on my own. As mentioned in the Sense of Smell and Taste chapter, interdependence becomes a critical aspect of functioning in the world around me. I feel strongly, however, about being accountable for everything I am capable of doing on my own, thus being as independent as possible and not always relying on others. Similarly, we taught the children at the school for the blind to understand that their own safety and self-reliance was an essential part of their education. It was paramount for them to use the skills they were taught so they could be accountable for their every step and move about in their environment safely.

The same goes for me. However, even in a sighted world, accidents happen. To avoid a mishap like running my knee into a table leg or missing a step and tumbling, it's *my* responsibility to use my skills to check things out before I put my body in motion. When I'm with another person and something happens, he or she often (unfortunately) feels responsible for the accident. Yet, it was my own fault if I didn't use the techniques I've learned. It's clear. I must be accountable for my own actions.

ᏍᎣ

All that said, feeling responsible for others does play a part in our lives. My sense of responsibility for another person kicked in during one of my trips through Chicago's O'Hare Airport. On January 16, while on my way to Lansing, Michigan, I encountered a huge storm that closed the entire airport. Not one plane was flying. That day, Chicago was as far as I could go for a while.

I was assisted to an area in the airport that had a TV and told I'd be called if any flights cleared. I got as comfortable as possible, pulled out my talking book, and settled in for a long wait. Occasionally, I removed my earphones and could hear the television turned to something like Wheel of Fortune. Because that didn't interest me, I listened to the conversations around me and could tell this waiting room was filling up.

Eventually someone sat down next to me on my left side. Engrossed in my audio book, I wasn't paying attention to my new seat partner. Before long, though, I took off my earphones and tried to get as comfortable as possible sitting in the airport chair.

"Lanshing?" The person on my left leaned into me. In quiet, broken English, she repeated, "Lanshing?"

I had no idea what she was saying. I finally realized she was trying to hand me something. I took the paper from her small hands and felt it to be her boarding pass.

"Lanshing?" I repeated. "Oh! Lansing?" I asked.

"Ya, Lanshing," she said again.

I figured out she was asking if she was in the right place for Lansing so I began to reassure her. After some time of trying to communicate, I realized she was Vietnamese and I could tell she was nervous. I'm also sure that, at first, she had no idea I was blind. There we were: I couldn't see and she couldn't speak English. What a pair.

Every now and then, the young woman said something to me and I tried to tell her to just wait with me. I did my best to let her know I was going to "Lanshing," too. Explaining that I was blind would have been fruitless, I thought.

Eight long hours after I'd landed in the snowed-in airport, a special assistance agent came up to me and said, "Mrs. Brock, come with me. We have a plane warming up for Lansing. There is a seat on it for you."

"Oh! Thank you!" I began quickly gathering my things. Weary and frustrated, I started to babble . . . "I have to speak at a conference tomorrow morning and I can't thank you enough." Suddenly, I felt a tug at my heart. I knew my Lanshing friend had no idea what was going on. I stopped and turned toward the direction of the person who had been my partner for the last five hours, then I turned to my escort and asked, "Is there another open seat?"

"Why?"

"This young lady doesn't speak English and I'm pretty sure she's going to Lansing, too. She's pretty shaken."

After all of those hours of sitting with her, I couldn't just leave her. Indeed, I felt a sense of responsibility for her. The agent paused, took a look at her boarding pass and said to have her come along, too.

"Come on, Lansing!" I said to her, using my arm as if I were directing traffic.

"Lanshing?!" she replied.

"Yes! Lanshing!" Now I was talking like her. With me on the agent's arm, we were moving quickly down the corridor, my new friend running behind, both of us with bags and purses in tow. We finally got to the gate where the plane was loading. The agent quickly punched a few buttons behind the counter as we bundled up to go outside. What a sight we must have been.

Going up the icy steps of the plane, I kept reassuring the young woman she was heading where she wanted to go. Then at the top of the steps, an airline attendant asked me, "Lansing?"

I almost cracked up.

"Yes, Lansing, and this lady is going there, too."

The attendant escorted me to my seat and my friend went to another part of the plane. Before departing, the wings of the plane had to be de-iced twice so it was shortly after midnight when we landed in "Lanshing." Thankfully, the meeting planners from the conference were at the airport to meet me. *I hope my little friend Lanshing had someone meeting her, too,* I kept thinking. I asked my contacts of her whereabouts, but they didn't see her. With all the confusion of arriving, finding luggage, and so on, I never knew what had happened to her. Yet my sense of responsibility prevailed. *I'm sure she has family she was visiting*, I kept telling myself. *I'm sure they were meeting her . . . I think . . . I hope.* Yes, I knew it was *her* responsibility to get where she needed to be. But I also like to think I helped her a little along the way.

꙳

For the most part, people are all wonderful in helping me, sometimes triggering treasured friendships. For example, in 1998, I was engaged to speak at a life insurance conference in Singapore. The trip would last four days and I knew several speakers on the same ticket for this International Million Dollar Round Table Meeting. I planned to fly through Dallas and, from there, through Tokyo. It had been arranged that a fellow speaker, LaDonna Gatlin, would join me in Dallas. This worried me because normally I have someone I'm familiar with accompany me when traveling overseas. But the meeting planners assured me Ms. Gatlin was agreeable to assist me with the help of the airline personnel. They didn't foresee any problem. Right. I sensed they didn't fully understand the complexity of it all. For one thing, I usually speak directly to the person I'll be with knowing that, at the very least, talking things through directly with the person is considerate. But this time, it just didn't happen.

In Dallas, LaDonna (about whom I knew more than she knew of me) joined me in the business class area of the plane. I had previously heard LaDonna present using her beautiful singing voice, and I was familiar with her famous singing brothers, the Gatlins. Not having spoken with her, though, I didn't know exactly what to expect and felt nervous about her having to help me. I suspected she had no idea what to expect either.

After switching a few people around, LaDonna and I were able to sit together. During the long hours flying to Tokyo, we shared much information about one another and the faith we had in common, becoming quick friends. However, before landing in Tokyo, I silently felt concerned about the "sighted guide" capabilities of my new friend. Guiding isn't something that falls into place immediately. I realized I had to take responsibility for my own issues. Of course, she was willing to help me with whatever I needed, but what might happen once we stepped off the plane couldn't be predicted. I knew we'd be testing how long this friendship would last!

The Tokyo airport was bustling, we were tired, and I had too much carry-on luggage. Weaving here and there, we prepared for a two-hour layover and I know we looked quite a sight. Not only was it a blonde leading a blonde but it felt like the blind leading the blind.

In the airport, LaDonna had the responsibility of taking care of me *and* figuring out where to go. Here again, I realized I had a better sense of direction than she, and we eventually found a good spot to wait. We were sur-rounded by people in a huge, crowded, echoing terminal with unfamiliar language filling the air. Before long, all the noise, confusion, and fatigue led us to laughing out loud.

Suddenly I heard what sounded like our names over the loudspeaker. "LaDonna! I think we're being called." I was right. LaDonna told me to watch the luggage (sure!) and she left me to go take care of things. When she came back, she said, "All I can figure out is they want us over at the counter."

We gathered our numerous belongings and headed there. Finally, we figured out that the agents wanted to know if I was capable of walking up stairs. Then they directed us to a gate area, with LaDonna leading me with her bag on one shoulder and one of mine on her other while I pulled my suitcase on wheels. Not long after that, we were escorted down a stairway, which is always scary for me. We walked outside and then stepped up into a crowded bus that had several levels. Finding some seats, we had luggage all over our laps and around our feet. It felt like we drove for a *long* time all squished together, with LaDonna filling me in on the happenings around us. When the bus finally stopped, I heard her gasp, "Oh my Lord! No wonder they asked if you could walk up stairs!"

Our plane was a 747. We had to climb an incredible number of stairs *outdoors*, again with our luggage in tow. It seemed like the stairs would never end. *They must be heading up to the clouds and into heaven!* I thought. Then, once we were in the plane, we climbed more stairs to reach our seats in the second story. By the time we sat down, we were exhausted and again in hysterics.

For LaDonna who had never been with a blind person before, this was a crash course in mobility lessons. Her sense of responsibility, however, and her enthusiastic desire to help me were never once in question. Being responsible is hard work; it takes tenacity and drive to get the job done. I can't tell you how many times I apologized for all the carry-on luggage I was dragging along. Not only did LaDonna have to guide *me*, but she had to make sure my bags made it through our transfer, bus and all, to our final destination. I must say I've changed my ways when it comes to packing.

My friendship with LaDonna continues to this day and our trip to Singapore provided us with wonderful memories. At the conference, we were inseparable. My favorite moment of all came when, during her presentation to the 3,000 Million Dollar Round Table agents, she sang "Amazing Grace" and dedicated it to me!

Sense of Responsibility in Our World

From the smallest of deeds to the huge efforts made by organizations, people are doing good things. World events, however, occasionally present issues that affect a multitude of people negatively. Too often, people point the fingers of blame at others. As an example, when the oil leak in the Gulf of Mexico occurred in 2010, many entities were responsible. The confusion of who needed to take action immediately became complicated but immensely important. For years to come, the courts of law and public opinion will still be assessing who acted responsibly and who did not.

The aftermath of the Gulf oil spill is only one example of how our world often shies away from doing the right thing. Are the responsible parties taking on the cleanup task and making it right, even when it hurts? Are those who have been affected by the oil spill being given opportunities to make good decisions on how to adjust? It's our responsibility to at least avail them with these options. We can accomplish this through our voices, our volunteer work, and our votes.

Your Insights into Sense of Responsibility

When you learn that being accountable for your actions is an obligation, then being responsible will strengthen your self-confidence. This comes with many rewards. The foundation for this sense starts at a young age: feeding the dog, making the bed, doing the dishes, and more. They all play a part in developing your sense of responsibility and belonging to a family. Forget about monetary payment; gaining a sense of responsibility and accomplishment is the reward.

Do those in your family have duties, jobs, and responsibilities they must take care of? If you were to assign tasks to each child, what benefits would follow? Adults often take over the task work because doing so is quicker. They even think they're helping by doing tasks for the children when, in fact, it hinders their growth and prevents them from developing their own sense of responsibility. In my childhood, the ways people modeled being responsible at my camp and beyond helped mold my understanding of this concept.

In the vision of the future you create for yourself, I suggest you build in a sense of responsibility within your faith, your family, your friends, your work, your community, and your country. Being accountable for your own actions will give you a lifetime of great reward. And once your goals are set and your tasks completed, then you will have left the "camp" better than you found it.

Sensitivity

"Today, I will commit one random act of senseless kindness ... will you?"
— Chuck Wall, Ph.D., Founder KindnessUSA.Org

I've been blessed to have had experiences with people whose hearts are filled with compassion. These people exhibit such gentle spirits they seem like angels walking among us. The following experience was so special for me that it became the first vignette I wrote for this book.

As sometimes happens when I travel, my flight changed and I was put on another airline. This day, I was flying through LAX (Los Angeles International Airport). When I landed, I was focused on getting to another terminal to catch the second leg of my original flight. I faced a long layover in Los Angeles.

As I deplaned, I was introduced to the airline assistant who would be my "eyes" for the next hour. On occasion, I can be concerned about trusting the stranger assigned to assist me. Little did I know how important *this* stranger would become to me.

"Hello, Miss. My name is Virgil."

The voice came from an elderly, very polite African-American man with language patterns that featured a southern drawl.

"Hello, Virgil. My name is Joan."

"Well, Miss Joan, how may I assist you this evening?"

I explained that if I could take his right arm at the elbow and he took my rolling suitcase with his left, then I could use my cane with my right hand.

"Yes, Ma'am."

At that point in my life, I don't think I'd ever been called "Ma'am." I instantly liked this gentle, proper man and the tone of his voice. Virgil proceeded to take care of business by looking at my boarding pass. Learning that we had to get halfway across this huge airport to catch my next flight, Virgil and I began walking toward the correct concourse. As I held onto his arm, I sensed he was smaller than my five-foot-nine-inch stature, but his aura was that of a regal and confident man.

"Miss Joan," he said, "we can call for a cart to transport you over to Terminal Two, or we could take a nice walk. It's a lovely evening in Los Angeles and I would be happy to escort you to your gate."

So we set out to walk. During those first few minutes, I couldn't help but notice how often Virgil was greeted by other employees saying, "Hi, Virgil!" or "How's it going, Virgil?" or "What's up, Virgil?"

As we strolled down the airport corridor, he asked about me, as usually happens. All the while, he greeted people by their first name or a nod of the head, which I could sense by his body movement.

"Virgil, you know *everybody* in this airport!" I declared.

He then explained he was the most senior skycap at the Los Angeles airport. I wish I could remember how many years he'd been working there; I just remember being shocked to hear the large number. Given his seniority at this point in his career, he could pick and choose the days and number of hours he wanted to work.

By now, we were outside strolling in front of one of the airport buildings, Virgil still acknowledging people as they passed us with a greeting. With cars constantly pulling up, the hustle and bustle of the curbside service was distracting for me. At one point, someone got out of a car and again, while dashing in front of us, greeted Virgil with a hearty hello. What an amazing number of greetings!

"Yes, Ma'am, that was Tommy Lasorda," Virgil said nonchalantly. I knew he was the famous manager for the Los Angeles Dodgers baseball team. I stopped on the spot.

"Are you kidding?"

"No, Ma'am," he replied. "Would you like to meet him?"

"Well, yes, but I wouldn't want to bother him," I said, feeling silly about abruptly stopping in my tracks.

"Not a problem. He's on the pay phone right now, but I know he won't mind." (This took place before cell phones were common.) After finishing his call, Tommy give Virgil a "hi" sign as he took care of some business. A few moments later, he came over and greeted the skycap with the warmest of handshakes and a genuine familiarity in his voice.

"Mr. Lasorda, this is Miss Joan," Virgil responded. "She wants to say hello to you." At that point, I could sense Virgil quietly backing away.

Tommy took my hand in both of his, focusing completely on me, and I nervously began to accomplish a task for which I never thought I'd have the opportunity.

"Mr. Lasorda, I just wanted to take this opportunity to thank you. A few years ago, your friend at the Air Force Academy called you and told you about a young man in Iowa who had cancer and just went through brain surgery. He was *born* a Dodger fan and the colonel asked if you would send him a photo or something. You very kindly took the time to write him a letter and send an autographed photo."

"Oh, yes, I remember this. He was a friend of the colonel's assistant."

"Yes," I said. "His name was Joe, and he was my husband. You have no idea what that meant to Joe and his family."

"I was glad to do it."

"Unfortunately Joe passed away, but your kind gesture was so appreciated, and that letter and photo are still treasured."

During this important exchange, the hustle and bustle

of the airport continued buzzing around us—horns blaring, people hailing cabs, skycaps helping their customers. Yet this noisy scene basically disappeared from my consciousness as Mr. Lasorda and I stood talking. Virgil politely stood nearby to assist me exactly when I needed him. Then Mr. Lasorda kindly wished me well and went off to the side where Virgil had been standing. He again spoke to Virgil for a brief moment and was on his busy way. It really was surreal.

After Virgil and I got back into motion, I thanked him for this valuable opportunity to show my gratitude to Tommy. Virgil responded by kindly telling me he, too, had lost his precious wife to cancer. In Virgil's touching words, I could hear the depth of loss. He missed his wife terribly. His pride shone through brightly when he spoke of their two wonderful children he'd put through college to become successful young adults.

Telling our stories and learning we were both Christians created an immediate connection between us. For both of us, our faith had been the support that had lifted our spirits through it all. It felt like I had known this man in a way that can only come through when sharing similar experiences.

Then our conversation circled in other directions when I asked Virgil if he'd worked with many famous people.

"Oh, yes, Miss Joan. I have seen them all."

"Who was your favorite?"

"Hmm. I suppose it might be the Duke, John Wayne

the actor. He was one of the nicest men. He was always so kind to me. I miss him."

My thoughts immediately flooded with memories of going to drive-in movies with Mom and Dad to watch those old John Wayne westerns. I felt a comfortable connection with Virgil and had fun asking him questions in the lovely night air. That easy stroll in the midst of our busy world had been more important to me than I could have ever imagined.

As Virgil left me at my gate, my mind's eye pictured this classy southern gentleman bowing as he said, "Miss Joan, this has been a mighty fine assignment for me. It has been a pleasure to be with you."

I was fumbling in my pocket for the tip I'd prepared to give him.

"Virgil, I only wish I could have you help me every time I fly through LA." I was trying to hand him the money.

"I wouldn't take your money ever," he replied in a most comforting voice. "God go with you, Miss Joan."

So I asked if I could give him a hug, which he graciously accepted. As he turned and walked away, I wondered how many planes he'd met and how many people he'd assisted in his lifetime. I felt as if I'd connected with one of the most inspiring people in Los Angeles—kind, professional, sweet, and sensitive to my needs. Years later, I suspect he isn't the senior skycap any more, yet the aura of his sensitivity and kindness that had touched my heart remains forever.

Sensitivity in Our World

When listening to the news reports on television, we hear of problems throughout our communities and in countries beyond our borders. Since the terrible tragedies of September 11, 2001 or 9-11, the hurricanes and countless other natural disasters that have occurred, reports emerging about people helping people are too numerous to count. As an example, right after 9-11, the *New York Times* printed a series of stories titled "Portraits of Grief." They featured accounts of the individuals who were lost in the terrorist attacks and others who helped those who were injured. From these stories, I concluded that being sensitive to one another in this desperate time was imperative.

How can we ever battle the evil that exists in our world? We see anger problems, abuse issues, terrible acts of violence, and multiple examples of hate every day. If we were able to eliminate this intense negative energy, then being sensitive to one another would become the norm. Yet, for the world to actually realize this change, it must start with each individual and expand until the kindness factor multiplies universally. No matter what level of difficulty we encounter in the struggle, ultimately we must strive to achieve sensitivity toward all.

Insights into Your Sensitivity

When is the last time you approached someone you labeled "insignificant"? Have you ever sat down with that person and asked about his or her dreams, hopes, or fears? As you walk through each day, consider stepping out of your comfort zone. Remember, your job isn't to fix others' problems or help them meet their goals. Rather, it's to show sensitivity to them in the context of the world *they* live in.

That's what I saw in Virgil. He exhibited the power of his kindness and sensitivity by doing the right "sensitive" thing with grace. When he asked me how *he* might assist me, he was being insightful in the most appropriate way. He wanted to know how to approach my needs. Virgil demonstrated opening his heart to others through kindness, gentleness, and an aura of calm and sensitivity. The great relationships he'd created with his colleagues awed me. I can only imagine his experience with his wife during her illness was difficult, but I suspect it was as positive and comforting as possible—because of his sensitivity. Add to that the kindness of Tommy Lasorda who had taken time to send a letter with a signed photo to someone he'd never met. Using thoughtfulness as they did, these kinds of gestures can be easy to do.

You never know how you can touch others' lives when meeting them. Once you've reached out to someone—just as Virgil did in his kindness to me—being thoughtful to others will come easier and easier. Showing this part of yourself is a powerful gift. Sometimes all it takes is listening with your full attention. As a result, you just may find yourself committing a random act of kindness. When you make the choice to be a sensitive person, your rewards will be many.

What is your most recent act of kindness?

PART II

The Senses We Need

B. The Senses That Test Us

Sense of Fear

"Don't worry about the world coming to an end today. It's already tomorrow in Australia."

— Charles Schulz

When I was a young child, I stood at my bedroom door, my hand on the light switch, my body poised in the start position to leap across the room directly into my open bed. If my acrobatic move was done *just right*, the boogie man under the bed wouldn't reach out and grab my foot! Once under the covers, I felt surrounded by the cloak of safety.

This unfounded boogie-man fear was invented in my young mind. Laughing at these immature thoughts while sharing them years later with college friends, we debated whether a spook really lived under that bed. My friend Mary said those dust bunnies on the hardwood floor under the bed were actually "spook poop." That was proof enough for her. How those innocent childhood fears can be so real to the immature mind!

While looking at dresses in a store one day (before

my vision loss), I took my eyes off young Joy for just one moment. Suddenly she was gone! Whirling around, I was looking, *looking*, LOOKING! A split second later, Joy's cute little face came peeking out from under a rack of clothes.

If you're a parent, you know the fearful feeling that can overwhelm your body with a surge that practically takes you to the floor. I was so frightened, I probably would have activated the Amber Alert child abduction bulletin had it been an option then. The second I saw her, I swept my little girl into my arms, closed my eyes, and hugged her tight. I couldn't even get mad at her. Visions of her being taken—of *losing* her—filled me with immense fear.

៚

I believe we can turn to education to ease our fears. Cliché though it sounds, knowledge is power—*and* a freeing tool. As mentioned earlier, when I lost my sight, I'd been teaching at the school for the blind for five years. From this experience, I had both *knowledge* and *information* about how to function as a blind person. Yet my sense of fear kicked in when I realized I'd have to buckle down, work hard, and practice for myself what I had been preaching. I had to *choose* to integrate the skills I'd been teaching into my own life. Could I do it? Did I *really* have the drive? That's what I was truly afraid of!

You can read the glaring signs when others feel uncomfortable in a situation. They laugh nervously or make statements showing they don't have a clue what's going on. When fear of the unknown is present, the nervous laughter can get carried away and even cause embarrassment.

An example from my family comes to mind. Mom and Dad married a few weeks after she'd graduated from high school. Dad had just finished seminary and immediately moved to his first church assignment in Iowa. Behind it, the country church provided a huge old parsonage and kind parishioners had planted a garden large enough to feed all of Des Moines. Taking care of that alone would have frightened anyone! As a homemaker, built-in choir director, and immediately pregnant minister's wife, Mom worked especially hard to do *everything* perfectly.

When I asked Mom how she dealt with all these challenges, she said she was too young to know enough to be afraid. But she did reach a breaking point of sorts. Early in their stewardship, a young mother in their area had died tragically. The entire community came to her funeral and Mom was a part of the women's trio singing during the service. She'd never performed music of this difficulty and admitted feeling a little afraid. On top of that, her nerves were raw and close to the surface.

During the funeral, the trio of singers sat on the stage behind the pastor, my father. The area was small and the women could look directly into the faces of the family in the front row—not a comfortable place to be.

At one point during the service when he needed more room, Dad scooted the pulpit chair back behind him with his heel. The motion pushed into the woman in the trio sitting next to Mom and caused her sheet music to fly! That's all it took. Mom got the giggles. She was a goner! Every time she thought she had her giggles under control, her nervousness caused her to start up again. What a terrible feeling! Mom could never tell this story without bowing her head in embarrassment and pausing for a repeat of the giggling. It reminded me of my favorite Mary Tyler Moore TV episode when Chuckles the Clown died. Mary, too, couldn't stop giggling at his funeral.

In the Sixth Sense chapter, I referred to the waving red flags in our stomachs and how they provide clues about what's really going on around us. This sixth sense partners with the sense of fear to create awareness. The day my mother found herself losing control at the front of the church, she began to understand that a person can *only do so much*. Because she was nervous, sad, tired, uncomfortable, immature, and, yes, afraid, this moment exploded on her. Thinking that the poor family would deem her to be insensitive at such a tragic time was especially awful to her. She had to accept her fears and vulnerabilities.

ॐ

Controlling one's reaction can be difficult—as Mom found out at the funeral—but applying what you know lets you go forward with a stronger sense of confidence.

When I think of fear involving physical danger, I revisit my time working at the mental hospital as a recreation therapist. There, I planned activities for a variety of residents, including the maximum security women.

Their stories were diverse, sad, complicated, and sometimes mysterious. For most of them, their physical stature
far outweighed mine and their minds were basically
destroyed. I had to learn not to underestimate the danger
of this situation.

A favorite activity for many of the patients was a
weekly bus ride. The hospital had acquired a used school
bus for outings and off-campus activities. One of our
endearing multi-impaired clients absolutely *loved* this old
blue school bus but couldn't pronounce the word "bus."
Instead, he called it Tuba and the name stuck.

One day as I stood at the door of Tuba, I watched the
ladies from the maximum security ward come shuffling,
strolling, and bouncing out of the large two-story stone
building. One of the two aides assisting me that day led
the group of thirteen. When she confidently walked up to
Tuba, she told me, "Joan, Dr. Z has given DeeDee the okay
to go on the bus ride today."

"Really?" I questioned.

"Yes. We'll watch her and if she gets agitated, I'll give
you a silent heads up and you can return us to the ward."

"Sounds good to me." As the driver of Tuba and the
one in charge, I liked having that all-important contingency plan.

I had worked with these two aides for several years
so I knew that *they* knew these patients as well as anyone.
DeeDee had a case history that especially saddened me.
She mostly stayed in seclusion. Among my activities with

her was getting her to speak calmly while throwing a Nerf ball to me in the lounge. In the previous three years, I had only seen her out of her building once or twice. However, I knew DeeDee had been improving and that this outing would be a big event for her. I felt happy to think how much she'd enjoy it.

One by one, each of the thirteen women took her seat—some by a window, some slumping and looking out, some sitting on the aisle portion of the old bench seat. The two aides sat directly behind the driver's seat where I was getting ready to go. From their position, they could look into the large mirror over my head and see activity throughout the bus. DeeDee sat in the second seat behind the aides.

I started up old Tuba, flexed my scrawny muscles, and clamped my hands onto the large steering wheel. We headed out on the road behind the dozen old huge buildings. I loved driving Tuba and this absolutely glorious spring day was perfect for taking a ride. But before we even left the compound, one of the aides caught my eye in the mirror and I saw her shake her head. DeeDee was rocking, rapidly looking left and right. We instantly knew this idea wasn't working for her. So at the exit, instead of turning left onto the road, I turned right to head back to the other entrance of the hospital on the horseshoe-shaped drive.

We were about two buildings from where we started when, all of a sudden, I felt a terrible pain in the back of my head. My hands flew off the steering wheel, my feet were pulled away from the pedals, and the bus stalled out! In lightning speed, DeeDee had lurched over the aides, grabbed my hair, and was pulling me over the back of my seat. My two colleagues jumped on her, one of them helping me lean back farther to release the pull on my hair and head. They got DeeDee to let go so I could sit upright in my seat. That's when I realized ol' Tuba had stopped within ten feet of the biggest tree I had ever seen. Scary!

While the aides quieted DeeDee, I quickly restarted the bus, backed it up, and headed for the maximum security building. Once we stopped, the aides exited with the poor woman who, by now, was reduced to a jelly-like calm. They disappeared into the building and I calmly sat in the bus with twelve mentally ill women. I turned in my seat and, rubbing the swollen back of my head, looked closely at my clients. To my amazement, none of them had reacted to DeeDee's outburst. Instead, they remained in their own positions of distant thought, still slouching or rocking in their seats. Surreal.

"Betty, are you okay?" I calmly asked one of them.

"Yes, Joan. Yes, Joan. DeeDee didn't want to go," Betty said quickly. She never made eye contact with me, just kept looking out the window at nothing.

"No. I don't think she did, Betty. Sal? How are you doing?"

"Fine," she said abruptly. "Will we go on the bus ride?" Sal, who always sounded mad, was in a continual state of agitation, but I'd never seen her react violently to anything.

"Yes. We just have to wait for the aides, okay?" I announced.

For some reason, I still don't remember feeling fear during this incident. Certainly shock might have been a factor because it happened so quickly *and* we focused on taking care of the business at hand.

It wasn't long before my colleagues came back expressing concern for me. I told them we still had a half an hour so let's just drive a little ways. They reentered the bus, I started up Tuba, and we commenced with the outing.

Later, after returning to my office building, I went to my supervisor and reported the incident. As a result, I was reprimanded for continuing the activity and sent home for two days. That's when my fear finally surfaced. In reliving this experience three decades later, I can still feel the fear that hit me *after* the fact. Was the decision to continue based on my immaturity? Did I have a false sense of security? Even today, however, I can't help but wonder about the pain and fear dwelling within DeeDee's sick, demon-filled mind. Somehow, she saw me as the enemy that day and, because of her fear, attacked the object of her focus. I propose that *her* chronic psychological sense of fear far outweighed any physical pain I might have experienced.

℘

I know that fear can be paralyzing and that facing our

fears demands honesty, courage, and resolve. When I lost my sight, my sense of fear wasn't about realizing I had to experience the world differently. Rather, I felt afraid about whether I would and could do it *positively*. Did I have the courage? Did I have the energy? Then when Joe died, the fears I experienced when I first went blind magnified tenfold. At that point, I especially feared that I couldn't keep a watchful eye on Joy and prevent her from being harmed.

Thankfully, through the demands of needing to "take care of business," all of my issues have worked themselves out. Similarly, I believe if you go forward with blind faith, life will always fall into place for you.

Sense of Fear in Our World

One morning, I tuned into a television talk show and listened spellbound to the results of a national survey. It revealed a list of the top five fears in our society. Here they are in reverse order:

5. Spiders

4. Public speaking

3. Snakes

2. Loss of sight

1. Loss of spouse

Thinking about my disability, my occupation, and my living in a desert, I realized I have a close affiliation with *all five*. Hmmm. This list could have put me in a desperate place, but I simply had to shake my head and not contemplate it too deeply. Over the years, getting on top of what each fear meant to me has allowed me to go forward without letting them control my chosen direction.

On the political front, our nation's leaders have wrapped our country in serious international confrontations that cause fear for everyone. I suggest it's prudent to educate ourselves and stay on top of important issues. We follow that process by voting in an informed way, which can abate some of the fear we feel. However, many people choose to stay out of it. They let their fears override their capability of handling the scope of what's going on.

Misinformation is often at the root of many fears, and a false alarm of any kind can be disconcerting. For example, on the eve of the new millennium—2000—many feared the world would be affected by technology breakdowns and shortages of all sorts. Thousands of people stockpiled water and food as a survival tactic. I say it's not bad to have back-up supplies in preparation for incidents that can happen. But in the case of that technology threat, the end of the world simply didn't happen—a false alarm. That tells us to be discerning when we listen to the misinformation that circulates around us or the fear it generates could overwhelm us.

Insights into Your Sense of Fear

I'm often asked if I felt afraid when I lost my sight. The question has caused me to study how fear can glaringly show up in one's personality. I've concluded that the following three categories of fear are the most prominent:

Immature or childlike fears—*usually unfounded and not based in fact.* After educating myself, experiencing and integrating the incredible techniques for the blind, I know now that the concepts I'd once carried about blind people were wrong. Once gaining knowledge corrected my inaccurate concepts, I could go forward in a positive, productive direction.

Emotional and psychological fears—*brought through the psyche.* My personal thoughts and insecure feelings often delayed my going forward in recognizing the many options I actually had for my future. After practicing and succeeding in every step of going forward, I was able to rest my mind about what I would be able to do.

Fear of physical danger—*caused by real experiences through life's journey.* I still struggle, and most likely will always be hesitant, when dealing with stairs, curbs, and other obstacles I'm not sure of. The falls and accidents I've experienced have rekindled that fear. It's something I must continue to work on.

During your children's formative years, your job as a parent is to help them balance the difference between the truths and the misconceptions of their fears. Early training in discerning truth molds a child's personality and builds strength and confidence.

As you grow and develop your own personality, this

complicated sense can show itself in feelings of anger, frustration, loneliness, disappointment, and even seclusion. For instance, when you encounter someone who is angry, you don't feel good being with him or her. That person's fear-based anger can evolve into bitterness—a feeling that's so destructive, it can eat you from the inside out like a cancer.

The many different emotions you experience when facing obstacles can roller coaster into different levels of fear. However, finding ways to cope with your feelings actually causes the obstacle to get smaller over time.

When it comes to coping, research has proven that walking thirty minutes a day can lengthen your life by several years. More important, exercise assists you through the stresses, frustrations, and fears of the moment. Breathing deeply releases tension and body stress in the middle of the day. Other life balance tools include reading, jogging, meditating, playing piano, swimming, practicing yoga, and more. These physical activities tone your day, your mind, and your soul, combining to bring positive productivity into your life. Finding your balance and the perfect fit for your life will help calm any fears you're struggling with. What is *your* life balancing activity of choice? How often do you use it?

Not knowing or being able to control what's around the corner can be difficult psychologically. After all, a sense of fear—sometimes small, sometimes large—lives within you throughout your life. But as you learn and mature from life's lessons, you become more capable of dealing with the unknown. And when you look back at moments that have taught you well, you'll be able to evaluate your own reactions and see how far you've come.

Whenever you find yourself fearing the "spooks" under the bed, work toward knowing that each and every day you can "fear not." This comforting truth will wrap you in a cloak of safety and bring you to a sense of peace.

Sense of Loss

"Blessed are they that mourn: for they shall be comforted."
— The Beatitudes, Matthew 5:1-11

My father and I were home alone one Saturday morning when the doorbell rang. He went to the door and greeted a young parishioner and his little girl. The man needed to speak privately with my dad. Being only ten at the time, I was delighted when they asked me to play with this three-year-old. Before long, we were surrounded by tiny little Barbie doll shoes and gloves sorted in piles.

After some time, the men came out of Dad's office. The stunning little girl with hair of shining ebony looked up and smiled at her daddy. Then my dad came over and moved in next to me on the living room floor where we sat playing. As he began talking to her, I looked over at the little girl's daddy and saw his ashen face. Even at my young age, I sensed something was terribly wrong. I later learned that this was the look of loss.

I only wish I could remember word for word what my father said to this precious child as he spoke to her. Mainly, he was saying that her mommy wouldn't be coming home again, that she'd gone to live with baby Jesus. He explained that, some day, all of us go see Jesus. But for now, she was to live with her daddy and everyone else in her family who loved her.

The mother's tragic death represented another sad loss in our church. I had seen my father prepare for many funerals like this one. In fact, I had helped my two older brothers clean up the church often. Being a preacher's kid, these kinds of things were expected and everyone chipped in. When I reflect on small memories like this, I realize how these powerful childhood moments prepared me for my own traumatic life experiences.

¡O

When my husband Joe died, he was thirty-six by only one day. It had been about five years since I lost my vision, and his illness lasted only seven months—an incredibly *long, short* seven months. Several weeks before Joe passed away, I was fortunate to have someone from the family with me at all times. My relatives drove or flew in from far-off locations to help with daily living and taking care of Joy while I stayed at the hospital with Joe during the cancer treatments. To get through each moment, each day, and each week, we adopted the Scarlet O'Hara attitude, saying we'll "think about that tomorrow."

On the day of Joe's funeral, our family made the long five-hour drive across Iowa to Joe's hometown of Vermillion in South Dakota. The next morning, we would bury him where he had grown up, where his parents still lived. We'd arranged for our pastor in Vinton, Iowa, to conduct the funeral services while my dad would follow up with graveside services. Clear memories came into my mind's eye of my father sitting, Bible in hand, penciling notes for the message he'd deliver. How often I'd seen this during my youth!

We stayed in one of the local motels, with Mom and Dad's room adjoining mine and Joy's. As I stood leaning on the pass-through doorframe in the hotel room talking with Mom, I heard the unmistakable sound of parchment pages of a Bible being turned. Even though I couldn't see Dad, I instantly knew what he was doing—finishing notes for his message the next day to bury my husband. What a powerful and poignant moment for me.

After saying our goodnights, I closed the door, leaned against it, took one of many deep breaths, and pushed away the huge lump in my throat. Joy was doing a room check, making sure both beds had the same bounce in their springs. During these difficult moments, this beautiful little eight-year-old had often balanced our days with the reality of the moment—the gift of her child's mind. Eventually she settled into bed. As Joy lay sleeping soundly, I went into the bathroom and started to run the water for a hot bath. My thoughts were scattered and I felt fatigued physically, mentally, and emotionally. After undressing, I began searching for the plug so I could fill the tub. I couldn't feel or find a rubber stopper anywhere.

The lever didn't stop up the drain either. I tried the lever again. Nothing.

In my tiredness, I turned to fetch Joe to help me find the plug. I stopped myself in my tracks. What had I almost done?! I stood there motionless, then slowly turned around and felt along the bathroom walls searching for the towel rack. Finding a washcloth there, I rolled it up tight, kneeled next to the tub, and stuffed it into the drain. The water level slowly began to rise and I carefully slid my weary body into the water.

When I relive this moment, it flickers across my mind in slow motion. We had been through *so* much in the previous seven months—*so* much in the last five years. Reality was finally hitting home. I felt sad, afraid, overwhelmed. Not until that moment did I truly realize *all* that had changed, *all* that I had lost, and *all* that I hadn't accepted. *So much had to be different going forward.* It was at that very moment I realized I still had losses I had to deal with. That included my vision loss.

How could it be that I hadn't dealt with this loss yet? After all, I'd been working at a school for blind children and had all the needed skills at my fingertips. I even had friends who were specialists in teaching the visually impaired. I just thought I should have been able to go on coping without any effort. *Of course,* I could go blind and not have it be a big deal!

Yet, Joe and young Joy had always stepped in to compensate. Together, we had made a silent pact to go on and not miss a beat. Denial had been my friend. But that night in the bathtub, this friend abandoned me.

Joe's cancer meant I had to face certain responsibilities and do them on my own. I hadn't, however, accepted that this scene would last *forever*. Secretly, I kept thinking the doctors were wrong, there'd been a mistake, and Joe would get through this illness. Yet *forever* is a complicated concept to understand. When I was first hospitalized, I had been told the damage to my eyes was *irreversible.* Looking back, I hadn't accepted this reality. It had been too hard for me to process. Indeed, it boggled my mind that a part of my body had *died* and could not be repaired.

Soaking in that "light bulb" moment of realization, I didn't cry, I didn't move. I just sat there in the tub, numb. My sense of loss was powerful. In my mind, I found myself reliving that childhood moment with the beautiful little girl whose mother went to see Jesus. It felt comforting, reassuring, and strangely encouraging for me to know that, the next day, my father would speak to all of us. I couldn't help but wonder if he'd ever thought about the moment in our living room telling the little girl her mommy wasn't coming home. I imagined all of Joe's family and friends being that little child sitting on the floor wanting answers. Dad would soon give them words of comfort and support through his message from God.

Even carrying a broken heart, I knew that, because of my fundamental beliefs, *I'd be fine.* I had to cling to that thought. I only wished each person who was mourning came away with that same realization. Did they also have a childhood memory to comfort them in this hour of need?

After climbing out of the tub, I lay down next to my sleeping daughter and took her small, soft hand into mine. The sound of her breathing, the familiar touch and size of her hand comforted me. Thankfully, I could feel my emotional and physical exhaustion giving way to sleep.

I have no idea how long I soaked in the tub that night. I only know it brought me to the moment when I understood that the loss I felt—that we *all* felt—was real. I knew I'd never be able to go back to the way it was, but I could go forward . . . for the sake of that little girl sleeping next to me.

Little did I understand in that moment that my resolve to go forward positively was for my sake as well.

Sense of Loss in Our World

Earthquakes, tsunamis, hurricanes, tornados, flooding from massive storms, and many more examples are tragedies we disbelieve have happened. These kinds of events can open our eyes to knowing that things are never in our control—not really.

However, during these powerful moments of loss, all around the world we see prayer vigils, people holding one another, and copious financial support and gifts. This happens even during the toughest of economic times. Where does that generosity come from? How does loss become such an important part of wanting to help and give?

Trying to reason through what tragic loss means is impossible. But when we find ourselves wanting to assist someone in need, a certain kind of growth and healing prevails that goes beyond rational understanding. These efforts prove to be essential in God's purpose as they provide hope for our world during immensely difficult times.

Insights into Your Sense of Loss

Your personal losses belong only to you. For example, the young person growing up on a farm sees the joy of kittens born, cows calving, and newborns clinging to their mothers; but there's a flip side. That child also experiences the death of favorite farm animals and the sense of loss that comes with it. If you recall your earliest lessons in loss, you can most likely correlate them with how you deal with your losses and the emptiness you feel today.

Life-altering changes come in many forms, such as losing your credit card, your house, your marriage partner, even something as extreme as losing a limb. Your goal becomes to turn each loss into productive action, making it your only direction of choice, your only option.

There is no good earthly answer to asking why you suffered loss. No one can tell you *not* to hurt, *not* to be sad, *not* to feel frustrated and out of control. These are normal human emotions. Facing reality, however, allows you to ward off any bitterness that lies around the corner.

During the duration of Joe's cancer, I still didn't face the reality of the little things—like writing checks to pay bills or getting Joy to her events or a million other tasks I had to take care of *on my own*. Yes, I had relied on Joe a lot during those first years of my blindness. Call me naïve, but his death forced me to realize I'd been living in denial for five years. Denial partnered with time is a defense mechanism that can buffer what's actually happening. But as I look back, I believe God gave me those five years as a gift to heal, learn, accept, and be prepared. I certainly didn't see it that way while I was in the middle of it all, but He slowly helped me to "fear no evil."

I also learned the importance of facing denial and getting my act together. Joe's death became *my* turning point—a time to stop and evaluate the lessons I'd been given. I urge you to carefully examine major turning points in your own life and ask, "Did I evaluate all the losses that caused me to stop in my tracks? Did I use denial to heal during those challenges? Have I ever put denial in its proper place and allowed my tragic losses to open my eyes to the work needed to move forward?"

Realize that these huge events of loss don't ever go away. As you remember them, you'll think of how it was. However, if you make the choice, little by little you'll go forward positively and productively. When you accept the reality that you can make this happen, it becomes possible to go through the changes, the challenges, and the unseen future in a productive and comforted way.

At the age of thirty-seven, I really *was* blind, and I really *did* lose my husband to cancer. In reliving my childhood, it became increasingly more evident that my best counseling took place *before* these life-altering events. Life's early lessons *can* help you through difficult moments if you pause to use all of your senses and reflect on what you've already learned.

In the midst of your loss, I encourage you to help others. Doing so is a strong anti-depressant that keeps you from wallowing in despair. Mostly, it takes the focus off what's happened to you. And it will reward you with the ability to pay back the help you have inevitably received during your own time of severe loss.

From the sense of loss comes positive action, but only if you *make the effort repeatedly.* Allow yourself to become that little child sitting on the floor. Let your faith in God reveal how He will help you. Yes, you *can* fill the void by putting your life in motion and living productively.

Looking at the whole picture can be overwhelming. That's why you want to surround yourself with loved ones and take change one day at a time. Use *all* of your senses in the coping process. When you find a way to "plug up the tub" and take time to heal, you'll be ready to deal with your sense of loss in a productive, life-affirming way.

Sense of Hope

"I geth all we can do ith hope."
— One of Joan Brock's students, 1984

The uplifting word "hope," even in its simplest defini-tion, exudes a positive feeling. It indicates calm and ease of life. Integrating this sense into our lives shows up in so many life stories that it's clear even the most deprived and lost cling to this natural survival instinct.

An example of how to go through the pain of healing before finding hope came to me when I was fresh out of college and working at the women's penitentiary, part of the state institution in Yankton, South Dakota. I was to accompany the inmates who had fulfilled their weekly requirements and could go over to the recreational facility. There, they were allowed to do whatever activity they wanted during the open recreation period.

When I got to the one-story fenced-in facility, only one client—a young woman in her twenties named Glenda—had met the requirements and was allowed to go. As Glenda and I walked together across the grounds, I could tell she was angry, upset, agitated, and tense. When I asked questions, her one-word responses made it clear she didn't want to chitchat. Just as we were approaching the back door of the building, I stopped and looked directly at her. Glenda stopped too and, toughening up her stance, looked at me with a definite attitude.

"What," she said defiantly.

"Look," I said. "Why don't you just scream?"

"What?" she asked, puzzled and disgusted.

"No, really. Just scream at the top of your lungs. No one is around, and trust me, you'll feel better."

"I don't need to," she snapped.

"Right. Whatever. I'll just step inside and you let it out, whatever *it* is. Then come on in." Then I turned and walked into the building. I suppose by leaving her unaccompanied for even that short time, I could have lost my job. But that young woman needed a release and some *hope* in believing there could be a light at the end of the tunnel.

It wasn't long before I heard a blood-curdling scream. I stood at the door facing in, smiling at the busy patients and staff moving around the room. After hearing the scream, a couple of my colleagues looked my way. I acted like nothing was wrong, just brushing lint from my coat sleeve. Soon, Glenda opened the door and stepped into the room.

"Thanks," she said under her breath.

"No problem."

Glenda asked if we could just sit in the smoking room

so she could have a cigarette. As she and I settled in, I carefully asked a few questions. She began to tell her story, opening the door to her life just a crack. Her words soon helped me see that before me sat a young, intelligent woman whose childhood and life's journey would have set *anyone* back on her heels.

I didn't talk much—just listened. I tried hard not to show my amazement at what she'd experienced at an age not much older than I was. How would I have turned out if I'd had a history like hers? Her choices had admittedly been bad ones, but her life examples had been even worse than her options. Clearly, we were different people with different backgrounds, but I like to think she could see me as a caring person in that moment.

After that day, Glenda eventually did better in her program at the prison. She and I had a different relationship after that, but we'd never be what we'd call "friends." Still, we both laughed when she'd come to me and say, "I think I just need to scream."

Glenda's quest for a sense of hope came through her own desires, tenacity, and positive choices. Gradually, she felt a sense of hope for a better future.

ᕽᑺ

Finding hope in the darkest of days can be difficult and confusing. Yet, pearls of wisdom can come into your life at the most unexpected moments.

After my lengthy hospitalization during the vision loss, I returned to work the day after leaving the hospital.

Previously, I'd been scheduled to take ten of the students to a peewee wrestling match about twenty miles away. Arrangements were made to have someone else drive, of course, and I was going as the chaperone. Before this abrupt change in my life, I would have handled it all on my own.

I vividly recall feeling nervous about walking back onto the beautiful old campus, built in 1852, where our school for the blind was housed. I'd seen the buildings day after day for five years. Suddenly I had to rely on my memory to picture a myriad of details so I could move independently around the campus. I *knew* I knew my way around, but did I know my way around as a *blind* woman? Foremost on my mind was envisioning the landmarks that would assist me in finding the front doors and the sidewalks. With so many confusing thoughts and fears circling within me, a desire to scream like Glenda did lay on the tip of my lips.

On the Saturday I returned to the school, the boys on the team and I were to meet at the entrance of their dorm. While standing at the entryway, I could feel the cold winter air on the outside. Then I heard the excited voices of the group of boys filtering down the stairs, a staff member in front of the pack.

"Oh, hi Mrs. B. We are *so* glad you're back!" he said.

"Thank you, Mike. I'm glad to be back, too."

"Are you feeling better?"

"You know, I really feel very well. Thank you for

asking, Mike," I said convincingly. I felt proud of myself for that!

Soon the boys surrounded me, giving their greetings and touching my arm as a way to wish me well. The ice had been broken. Then the van pulled up and Mike assisted the boys into the vehicle. At the back of the pack was eight-year-old Terry. He was standing next to me when he turned to me, looked up to hear my voice, and touched my hands.

"Mitheth B? I'm really thorry to hear about your vithion loth, but I geth *all* we can do ith hope."

Terry's words were filled with immense sincerity. His precious lisp simply filled my heart to overflowing. He was an adorable young boy with the most stunning prosthetic eyes I'd ever seen. I had lost my sight in a three-week period and knew I'd likely never see again, but *I had been able to see* for thirty-two years. Terry had *never even seen* his own adorable face—not once—and he never would. Yet this little boy was still clinging to hope for . . . whatever.

It was the most important thing I needed to hear at that moment. If this little boy could feel a sense of hope, then so could I.

Standing with my young student after his sweet words of hope, I suddenly realized the driver was honking at us from the school van. Terry and I walked down the sidewalk together, me with my new white cane, and he on my right arm.

"So, are you going to win your wrestling match today, Terry?"

"I *hope* tho, Mitheth B."

Sense of Hope in Our World

Trying to analyze events in the world that have no justification is complicated. Why are so many killed in a tragic hurricane, flood, earthquake, or blizzard? Why do terrible things happen to us? Why can't we figure out the cure to cancer? Why can't we truly find peace in the world?

The massively heavy questions we ask will never end. We often have trouble comprehending the answers given. Instead, the result must be in finding a way to contribute what we can to help the causes that concern us most now.

What I find genuinely impressive is all of the organizations and groups that offer hope to the poor, the needy, and the lost. Do we need to do better? Yes. Are there many more people who need help than are being served? Yes.

Yet, the fact remains that we have more giving people in the world than is generally known about—including those who contribute without asking for recognition. They contribute just because they can. This encourages us to give more in the future.

When a concerning issue comes to our attention, the answer is always to take action. In this way, we can truly help to give hope to others in our world.

Insights into Your Sense of Hope

I've always been blessed to have a strong foundation of love from my family and friends. But when my life changed, I knew it was up to me to take all that I'd learned, lived, and taught, and to integrate it into my life while preserving my own sense of hope. The ball was in my hands. I had to make good choices and *get on with it*.

I have early memories of hoping for a pony under the Christmas tree. Was that realistic? No. Our family lived in a city and didn't have a place to board a pony. Still, each Christmas, I thought it *might* happen. Silly? Yes. Disappointing? Definitely. But maturity helped me to understand better.

From the dream of owning a home to the hope of a raise in salary, people experience the sense of hope every day. What hopes and desires do you have? Are your hopes more realistic than wanting a pony at Christmas? Are you setting yourself up for failure? The minute something difficult happens, do you tend to lose hope? If so, what inner part of you allows that to happen?

Realizing it or not, you experience this sense *every day*. It's what keeps you going. When you lose hope, you falter, perhaps failing to forge forward in the midst of life's difficulties. I suggest keeping your mind healthy with positive facts and experiences, and keeping your body healthy, too. That will help you get through the tough stuff—including the levels of healing you must go through when traumatic change strikes.

In meeting people all over, an enjoyable part of what I do is entertaining questions about how I've handled difficulties in my life. The most commonly asked question involves how I dealt with the anger I felt. I typically reply, "When you allow anger to sink into your soul, you will become bitter. When you are *bitter,* you will not get *better.* And worst of all, you lose hope."

Although, you can find a positive path to this hope by allowing yourself to experience the *difficult* feelings—the frustration, sadness, loneliness, disappointment. These and other negative feelings become part of the all-important healing process.

In fact, going through a maze of emotions is normal *and* imperative. If you can release them appropriately, then you're developing a step-by-step method for moving forward as a result. Whether you pound the pillow or scream at the birds outside, you're releasing tension that can fester in your soul, just as an infection can rot a wound.

So look into your heart. Are you bitter? Have you allowed yourself to heal through all of the disappointments and obstacles you've experienced? Are you harboring a bitterness that slowly eats at your soul? If so, this may be hindering you from living with hope.

In all of my daily tasks of *getting on with it,* help always surfaced. I only know that as I look back on those early days of extraordinary change, I discovered that often the smallest moments supplied the largest gifts of inspiration. Remaining alert and aware to those around you, you will see the messages that are given to you through others—as I did through young Terry's encouraging words of hope to me.

It's definitely easy to lose hope during extreme events. When my vision loss was new, knowing I'd live in a mono-chromatic world gave way to finding it hard to make any sense out of *anything* around me. But the simple words of a young boy one day put it all into perspective for me.

Yes, your sense of hope can come from the most innocent. When you run into one of those life-altering moments, you might have someone like Terry to lift your spirits up and over the obstacles. And if you tune in to all your senses, you won't miss or disregard the precious messages of hope that will magically come your way.

Joan and Jim ready for a
black tie dinner during a 2006
Mediterranean cruise.

Sense of Peace

"And on earth, peace, goodwill towards men."
— Luke 2:14

While sitting in my office writing this book, the ringing of an ice cream truck's bell came floating through the quiet of our neighborhood. This sound brought back childhood memories and transported me to a secure, warm place of peace. In reflecting on all of the incredible experiences I've been given, I strive to find a balance in how they've played a part in my gaining a sense of peace over the years.

Certainly, one of the most important moments for me was the last time I said goodbye to Joe. Early on the morning of Joe's funeral, I went to the church with my father and my eldest brother Bob to make sure everything was in order. Only a few people, including Joe's loving father, had come for the short final visitation, which had been previously announced. After we shared emotional hugs and poignant words, they said goodbye to Joe and left shortly after.

Now it was my turn. Bob and Dad went up to the front of the church with me, then walked away. I found myself alone, standing next to Joe in his coffin. I could smell the sweetness of the flowers in the immense silence of the church. Then I slowly reached out and touched Joe's arm. I know that making this gesture may be difficult for some to understand, but for me as a blind person, it was an important way to share this final time alone with him.

The calm of the moment overwhelmed me as I acknowledged how bravely this young man had fought and, his struggle with cancer now over, how he finally found peace. Thank God. In my heart, I knew that all of us—his family, friends, students, and doctors—had done everything humanly possible to support him in beating this ugly disease.

The quietness filled my soul with peace and I held onto it as long as I could. I realized that, before even attempting to go forward with my life, I had needed this powerful private moment with Joe.

When I felt ready, I turned and walked toward the back of the church. Touching each pew one by one brought me closer to understanding the reality of what had happened—and of what needed to happen next. I knew right then I had to take responsibility for organizing my life, *our* lives, so Joy and I could head in a positive direction without Joe.

As I reached the back of the church, I listened for the voices in the entryway and paused. Then I calmly turned to look back at the empty sanctuary one more time. No, I couldn't see it, but my mind's eye recreated the sight I'd seen in years gone by. I could feel the emotion of the room and wondered where our lives would go next—where we'd end up belonging.

The familiar scent of the church comforted me. Soon it would be filled with family, friends, students from the school for the blind, and loved ones with whom we'd shared life and laughter. In my heart, I still felt the peace from my last touch on Joe's arm. At that moment, I put my fear into the palm of my faith. I could now lift my head toward the future.

I wiped away the taste of tears from my cheeks as I turned to leave the entryway. My father came to my side, lifting me out of the private world I had been in. He sensitively asked, "Joan, are you okay?"

"I am."

Then Bob came up, put his arm around me, and asked, "Are you ready to go?"

Taking a deep breath, I replied, "I am now." Feeling a firm foundation of family support in this powerful moment uplifted my spirits and brought me a sense of peace.

❧

After Joy and I moved back to Bakersfield, I bought a small condo with a lovely patio. My brothers Bob and Jon, with their wives Chris and Kala, purchased two gardenia plants as a housewarming gift. Because they knew it was my favorite fragrant flower from the region, I regarded it as a thoughtful welcome to our new start. One day I sat in the shade to soak up the late afternoon summer warmth while Joy played with neighborhood kids. I breathed in the fabulous scent of these delicate flowers and thought, *So much has happened!*

Suddenly I realized my mind had gone totally blank — not one thought in my head. For so long, I had so much to organize, so many appointments to meet, so much to think about, so many people to talk with, and so much to be responsible for. At this moment, finally, I had nothing to do. With my body calmly at rest in my chaise lounge, my senses filled with old fragrances — and new realizations. Ah, peace!

That's when I knew that turning to all of my senses would be the avenue to completing the picture of each and every day. And being in this awareness would be the path to living with a sense of peace.

✿

To continue my quest for living peacefully, I had much to take care of. First, I had to come to an understanding that I wasn't in control of every facet of my life. Accepting this fact was, and still is, a daily task for me. I acknowledged that taking the initiative to forge through these changes was, in fact, the only thing I had control over. Curling up into a ball or burying my head to avoid dealing with life would never bring me peace. I simply had to jump over lots of hurdles. That's when I committed to writing about all of my experiences, including my losses. Painful though it was at times, reliving them proved cathartic; writing about them has allowed me to move forward.

Today my peaceful moments often come when I have called or spoken with all of the important people in my world and know they are safe—especially Jim, Joy, Brian, my grandson, and others I know and love. Only then do I feel the most at peace.

Sense of Peace in Our World

How often have we heard the phrase "can't we all just get along?" It may come with a humorous slant, but doesn't it also ring true?

Since the beginning of time, we've seen disharmony enter almost every facet of life. As we frequently witness the conflict between countries, finding the balance of working together despite our differing beliefs and traditions can be an ongoing struggle on our path to peace.

In 1960, President John F. Kennedy launched a federal agency known as the Peace Corps. Through this organization, a wonderful group of giving people still serves our country in the cause of worldwide peace. Volunteers live and work in developing countries, devoting themselves to promoting peace and friendship. Over the years, the Peace Corps has helped millions of people build a better life for themselves, their children, and their communities. Similar efforts are seen in many other organizations and religious groups that help people with education, medical assistance, and community-building.

I've learned that finding peace in our world starts with one person at a time, one task at a time, one goal at a time. From these actions comes a sense of peace that only those who offer their gifts can feel.

Insights into Your Sense of Peace

James Taylor's beautiful song "Secret O' Life" is one of my favorites. As I focus on the encouraging words of finding a way to enjoy your life, while wrapped in the songwriter's beautiful melody, I experience a lovely sense of peace in the moment. So often music does this for me.

Are *you* enjoying your life? Are you feeling a sense of peace? What is your most peaceful moment in each day? What is your most memorable experience of feeling peaceful? Do you write about these in a journal?

When given the opportunity to walk along the seashore, I experience the amazing sounds of the waves lapping and the seagulls squawking. As I feel the wet sand oozing under my feet, I sense a peace that feels healing to me. Can you recall an experience that does this for you? Do you allow moments of peace into your day, week, life? How can you use your own sense of peace to clear your head and balance everything in your soul?

As you search for that sense of peace, take a deep breath, lean on your faith, family, and friends, and act like a peacemaker. How? You can start by journaling your thoughts and feelings.

Using your senses to relive life events and then putting words on paper demands that you stare every significant happening in the face. Writing organizes your thoughts and assists you in evaluating how you have dealt with, felt about, and reacted to those key life events. Undoubtedly, you'll find the ugly moments hard to relive but, still, write about them as best you can. Doing so assists you in coping better than you ever have.

In your search for peace, I suggest you combine journaling with other healing tools. When you treat yourself from that ice cream truck going by, you'll heighten the possibility of enjoying and finding peace in your life.

CONCLUSION

And So It Continues . . .

"Life can only be understood backwards, but it must be lived forwards."
— Soren Kierkegaard

The downward spiral of a dear friend of mine and how she finally dealt with her circumstances powerfully portrays how one can tough it through and move forward. After a difficult divorce, my friend found herself responsible for the children, a large home, and land to take care of. To keep her head above water financially, her professional responsibilities took priority.

Several years later, after her children were grown and gone, she found herself living alone. Sadly, she'd let her three-bathroom home fall into disrepair. When one bathroom broke down, she just moved to another. Eventually, all three bathrooms as well as the kitchen sink fell apart. The confusion of life had taken control; she was finally forced to "see" the problems.

After a scan of the Yellow Pages by my friend, enter a small, Italian-born, elderly plumber with a clipboard and pen in hand. She led him around the house, showing him what needed to be repaired. He finally stopped, looked at her, and crossed his arms with the clipboard across his chest and under his chin. Then he put his other hand on his right cheek and shook his head. With a gentle, accented voice and a tinge of sadness, he asked, "Why you wait so long?"

She had no answer.

In two days of laboring long hours, this sweet, hard-working man put her house back into working order. He went above and beyond by fixing little things he noticed on his own. As he headed out to his truck on the last day, he looked at my friend and said, "You no worry about the small things now."

After sharing this story with me, my friend and I were determined to discern why it did take her so long to deal with these issues in her home. Her most important lesson, she decided, was simply failing to reach out for help when she needed it. With the will to face all the problems that had to be fixed buried deep in her heart, setting a plan in motion for repairing them over time became her new goal.

❧

During the loss of my sight, my childhood buddy Louise called me often during my hospitalization. She told me how helpless she felt and how she wished she could do *something, ANYTHING!*

"Can't I come and just clean your toilets or something?!" she begged. From thousands of miles away, she believed her hands were tied.

While experiencing that helpless feeling of wanting to do *something, ANYTHING,* she called and recited a poem to me. This simple gesture turned into more of a gift than she ever could have known. The poem comforted me then as it does today. I have often shared it with my audiences and have had many requests for it. I hope it will touch your heart as well. I tip my hat to the unknown author.

I am the light where God shines through,

For He and I are one, not two.

I will not fear, nor fret, nor plan;

He wants me where and as I am.

And if I be relaxed and free,

He'll carry out His plan for me.

Our World

The historians can pull together many world events, present them, and show how history repeats itself. To go forward and continue our lives in an upward motion, it's prudent for us as a society to study the lessons we have learned.

A popular concept called "pay it forward" suggests that when we benefit from something somebody does, we do the same or something similar for another, thus paying forward the gift. People helping people creates the foundation for getting us through the tough stuff. Compassionate actions and generosity can truly give hope to those in our world who need assistance and encouragement to continue.

Your Insights

The Road Less Traveled by M. Scott Peck begins with the simple words "Life is difficult." I must repeat, I'm an ordinary person to whom extraordinary things have happened. I grew up in a faith-based family, which has been instrumental for me in getting through the toughest days of my life. I'm a different woman today than I was yesterday, and I will become a different person tomorrow. And yet I am the same. Each choice, mistake, experience, moment, and landmark that I have experienced has molded me, as yours have molded you.

All of my senses have influenced those incidents and I consider them to be gifts from God. I wish I could say I have always used all of my senses to their fullest, but I haven't. I am still learning. And that's the point.

Your cornucopia of senses helps you grow and learn with every landmark. Your core comes from your own layers of experiences growing up; they rally to give you an overall sense of being, thus creating the essence of who you are today.

I've often been asked about the appropriate thing to do when someone you love has gone through or is going through struggles, losses, or tragedies. I only know what helped me and what I've been able to do for others. Here are just a few actions that will always mean a lot.

It was never too late to receive a card.

Hugging me helped and words were not always necessary.

The only "wrong" way to support someone is to do nothing.

Listening can be valuable when someone needs a sounding board. For example, listening to my girlfriend's plumbing problems was my only way of being there for her. I couldn't fix the problems and I'd never been through a divorce so I had no advice to offer from experience.

And remember, if you're on the receiving end of all this support, acknowledge those steps you've taken on your own. Each one has given you knowledge and experience to help you develop who you are. What invaluable moments!

❦

In seeking ways to express your caring, I ask you to find your own voice. I would not be where I am today were it not for *all* of those voices around me who shared their wisdom. Their incredible gestures of love continue to this day. As mentioned earlier, I'm blessed to come from a loving and supportive family. I wish that to be true for each person who struggles. Laying the firm foundation of a family unit is critical to strive for.

My daughter has been and continues to be the light of my life. This light now includes her husband Brian and a precious grandson Skyler. Jim, my Butterfly Man, supports and encourages me through his amazing love, patience, and understanding. The circle of other family members and friends I have shared stories about provides examples of what you, too, have at your fingertips.

If you find yourself waiting too long to take care of business—to handle or repair what's going wrong in your life—possibly a little old Italian plumber, an angel in disguise, will come into your life and put things into their proper perspective. Beat him to the punch and ask, "Why *do* I wait so long?" Realize that when things break down emotionally, physically, or relationally, ignoring the issues without fixing them only hinders you from moving forward.

Instead, focus on coming to your senses and using all of them. In this life quest of living positively and productively, you can see the multitude of senses that give you a life of joy—*if* you make the choice to see them. And as you advance in your quest, I send you off, encouraging you to take that much needed walk on the beach, repeating the same thing Virgil, my Los Angeles skycap, last said to me:

"God go with you."

ACKNOWLEDGMENTS

"A person is a person through others."
— Anonymous

I want to honor the people who have encouraged me, advised me, laughed with me, cried with me, educated me, driven me around, inspired me, shopped with me, brainstormed with me, worked with me, prayed with me, and loved me. We simply do not do life alone.

By listing the following names, I risk leaving someone out, but each of you knows what part you have played. Know that I treasure all of you.

My immediate family: Jim Brock, Joy, Brian, and Skyler Glasco, Bob and Chris Stuebbe, Jon and Kala Stuebbe, the wonderful Brock contingency, the loving Glasco family, and all of my extended family members. Thank you for that continued foundation of family, love, and support.

In addition, the following family members and friends inspired me in a multitude of ways while I was writing this book:

Brenda Armstrong, Steve Bauer, Judy Bolt, Rhonda Chaney, Scott Clare, Stan Cooper, Mary David, Gail Davis, Bert Decker, Carol Deschens, Mimi Donaldson, Marguerite Ensio, Louise Erreca, Neale Godfrey, Paul Goff, Bonnie and Dr. Lou Greco, Larry Grypp, Julie Gunther, Grace Horn, Dewitt Jones, Jim Knipper, Carey Lowell, Sandy Morris, Patty Pearson, Ronald Price, Ann Reick, Pastor Mark Roessler, Susan Rogers, Kay Schieble, Linda Schultz, Mike Shaw, Lisa Shearin, Dr. Robert Snyder, Jan Stuebbe, Tom Sullivan, Dian and Dr. Lane Tassin, Kim Turner, Chuck Wall, Evelyn Wegis, Deb Wilberg, and Jean Williams.

Joy, Brian and Skyler's first family portrait!   Being a grandma is the best! 2012

Thank you also to the following special people who played a direct part in the creation of this book:

The incredible staff at Wheatmark Inc. Your professionalism, kindness and special efforts have meant so much.

Barbara McNichol for your professional advice and

beautiful editing. You have helped make this book what it needed to be.

Mike Bremer for the beautiful Foreword, your early editing, advice, and support on how to organize this book.

LaDonna Gatlin for your constant cheerleading.

Jill Ives for the many hours during the early years of research, technical assistance, and brainstorming.

Mary LoVerde, whose encouragement, support, and endless connections have been more valuable than I can describe.

Jillian Manus and Penny Newman, whose encouragement and insights opened my eyes to what this book could be.

Mark Mayfield for your expertise and talent in assisting me in relaying my humor on the printed page.

Hannetjie Pietersie, photographer, who took my photograph for the back cover.

Connie Ronstadt, whose time, talent, and insight helped make it all happen.

My trainers and counselors of technology for the blind: Janet Dylla, Gayle Fisher, Kaye Hunt, and Bea Shaperro. What an amazing sense of timing! This book couldn't have been accomplished without your guidance, support, and expertise.

Thank you all for believing in me and allowing me to use your eyes.

ABOUT THE AUTHOR

At age thirty-two, Joan Brock suddenly lost her eyesight to a rare eye disease. Only five years later, she lost her first husband to cancer. Gaining wisdom and courage through her losses and choices, she now shares how she overcame adversity and inspires those who have experienced losses to "get on with it." A speaker for more than two decades and now the author of two books, she has traveled around the world with her poignant presentation and insights into coping positively and productively.

Joan's autobiography *More Than Meets the Eye* was published in 1994 by HarperCollins and made into a Lifetime television film in 2003 with Carey Lowell starring as Joan. The film continues to be replayed nationally as well as internationally.

In *Come to Your Senses,* Joan again takes you on an insightful journey. She shares moments of her life that brought her wisdom through the many and varied senses she still retained. These moments are spiced with memories from her sighted days as well. Her stories encourage you to evaluate your own life path and live it to the fullest by using all of your senses—physical, mental, emotional, and spiritual.

Joan lives in Tucson, Arizona with her husband Jim. Her daughter Joy, son-in-law Brian, and grandson Skyler live nearby, a blessing she appreciates each and every day.

*For more information regarding Joan's books
and speaking career, please visit www.JoanBrock.com*

"Do it from the heart, Honey."
— Jim Brock, Sense of Touch chapter